THE
MORTGAGE
COACH

JOEY SHEAHAN

THE ULTIMATE GUIDE FOR FIRST-TIME BUYERS AND HOMEOWNERS TRADING UP OR SWITCHING MORTGAGE

MERCIER PRESS

Waterford City and County
Libraries

The only thing that matters is what we do next!

Joey Sheahan

MERCIER PRESS
Cork
www.mercierpress.ie

© Joey Sheahan, 2020

ISBN: 978 1 78117 738 9

A CIP record for this title is available from the British Library.

Printed and bound in the EU.

CONTENTS

ABOUT THE AUTHOR

With over twenty years' experience in the property and financial services industry in Ireland, Joey Sheahan has provided thousands of people with mortgage, property, life insurance and pension advice and services. He has been involved in deals totalling half a billion euro over the past two decades.

Joey has always been a self-starter with a strong appetite for commerce. Following five years working as an auctioneer, he founded MyMortgages.ie in 2005, which has gone from strength to strength ever since – navigating some tricky economic waters and emerging as one of Ireland's most respected and renowned brokerages with a national presence. The business has grown steadily year-on-year and Joey is committed to ongoing growth in the years to come.

It wasn't a surprise that his career path led him to the mortgage and financial services sector. His father, Frank, an auctioneer and property developer, introduced his children to the world of property at a young age and Joey spent his summer holidays working on building sites from the age of twelve. It is to Frank that he gives credit for instilling in him a hard-working and honest approach to business.

Joey has an instinct for business and a natural rapport with people – and both attributes have contributed heavily to his achievements over the years. He is an active advocate for charities and community initiatives, and a willing participant in fundraisers that range in scale from 5k runs to marathon, triathlon and open-water swimming events.

A seasoned rugby supporter and player, Joey still keeps a firm footing in the sport. A few of his highlights include captaining the Presentation Brothers College Cork team to victory in the Munster Schools Junior Cup, winning a Senior Cup medal, followed by winning the 1998 U–19 Rugby World Cup with Ireland and the Students European Cup with UCC in 1999. He represented Ireland at U–19, student and university levels. He says that these sporting successes 'made me believe that I could achieve anything from a young age'.

He may have since hung up his boots as a player to settle for the comfort of the stands, but his experiences from that time have had a formative and lasting impact on his attitude to teamwork and leadership.

This book is a culmination of years of hard work, dedication and enjoyment, so don't delay – get stuck in!

TESTIMONIALS

'It's all about people at the end of the day. I know just how momentous it is for clients when they walk through the front door of their new home for the first time. It can be a milestone moment in their lives and the culmination of hard work and effort. Most often, it's the realisation of a dream come true. So the acknowledgements the team receive are always appreciated and reflective of how much we become part of each client's mortgage experience.

'I have worked with MyMortgages.ie over the last six years and would strongly recommend them. My broker Joey is efficient, quick to understand the current financial situation, and continues to assist with finding new ways to help save money as well as the best deals for his clients. Joey works well to find the right solution for each client, which is key today.'

Rachel Maher, Talent Acquisition Manager

'A sincere thank you to Sinéad, Siobhán and Joey. You have all made this process so easy for us. Thanks to you and the team, we will be moving into our new home a lot sooner than we ever thought. You took all the stress out of the process, keeping us informed every step of the way. It was evident from the very beginning that the team at MyMortgages.ie was working with our best interests in mind and delivered exceptional service from start to finish. I honestly do not think we would be at this stage without the help you have all given us along the way. It's greatly appreciated.'

Alison Walsh, Wedding Planner

'A sincere thanks to Joey, who was recommended by a friend of mine. Your exceptional knowledge and efficiency made it possible to purchase our first home at the best interest rate and structure that really suited our individual needs. We will be using your services again in the future!'

John Riordan

'Joey and the team were very helpful throughout the application process for our second home. We felt very comfortable with the decisions made and knew from the first conversation that we were in safe hands this time round. We have recommended MyMortgages.ie to numerous colleagues and friends.'

Dr Dominic O'Sullivan

'Myself and my partner decided to buy a house this year. Unexpectedly, a house that was ideal for us came up before we had mortgage approval. We contacted Joey in MyMortgages.ie and we submitted a mortgage application straight away. Joey was able to assure the auctioneer that our mortgage approval would be a formality even before we were formally approved. On this assurance we were allowed to bid on the house. Luckily, we went sale agreed the same day the mortgage approval arrived.

'Being self-employed we had a few more hurdles than usual

to overcome, but Joey and his team made the process as stress-free and straightforward as possible. Would highly recommend.'

Pat Fitzgibbon, Musician and Broadcaster

'Unhappy with my interest rate, I had read about people switching their mortgage lender and making significant savings, so I made enquiries at MyMortgages.ie and was so impressed with the team, who answered all my questions. I now have a much better interest rate and the whole process was so organised and efficient. The team are highly skilled at determining the client's position and making the appropriate recommendations.'

Michael Fitzgerald

'We came to MyMortgages.ie in the midst of a complicated and protracted process of mortgage application through our bank. Exhausted and frustrated by the ongoing nature of dealing with the bank, we approached MyMortgages.ie. We instantly found ourselves at the centre of a process that we were being supported and guided through, as opposed to being on the outside of the process with the bank. We submitted our information to MyMortgages.ie and were never asked for that same information again and again as we were with the bank. We were given a clear timeline and a clear set of expectations. All of our queries were answered immediately, all of our concerns were allayed and MyMortgages.ie delivered ahead of every deadline. Joey, Tim, Sinéad and Siobhán were clear, efficient and knowledgeable from the get-go! While the relief of finally having the correct paperwork in our hands that allowed us to move to our next home was immense, the ease of dealing with MyMortgages.ie and their informed style of open communication was equally as immense for us. We highly recommend MyMortgages.ie and wish them every success in their future business!'

D. and A. McCarthy

'As first-time buyers MyMortgages.ie were recommended to us by friends. Having spoken to Joey, Siobhán and Sinéad we were in no doubt that MyMortgages.ie were the best option for us. The team really took the stress out of the process of purchasing our home. They provided a friendly, diligent service from our initial application right up until we got the keys to our new home. What really set them apart was their personal touch and we really appreciated this. In turn, we have highly recommended MyMortgages.ie to numerous friends looking to buy their own home.'

Paul and Laura

'Myself and my wife took out a mortgage through MyMort- gages.ie in 2015. We were paying €1,400 per month and were too busy to review our interest rates. Out of the blue Joey contacted us and informed us that the bank we are with had dropped their rates. We entered into a two-year fixed rate of 2.3% without having to apply for a new mortgage, which saves us €260 p/m or €3,120 annually. Joey and his team were very efficient and professional throughout the process and we would highly recommend MyMortgages.ie as they didn't forget about us even after we bought the house.'

Lyndsey El Amoud

'We would like to extend our sincere gratitude to Joey and the team in MyMortgages.ie for all their help. I spoke with Joey two years ago about getting myself and my family into a position for a new mortgage. We are so grateful for his time, honesty, experience and professionalism. Sinéad and Siobhán organised all our necessary requirements and they were nothing short of amazing. I could not recommend MyMortgages.ie any higher.'

Andy and Brenda

'I recently saved €4,800 per annum by switching my mortgage through MyMortgages.ie. I didn't realise that switching your mortgage is far easier than the initial mortgage when purchasing a property and that the Central Bank loan-to-income and loan-to-value exception/exemptions don't apply for switchers.'

Daragh McSweeney

'We are originally from Ireland and have been living in Dubai for the past three years. We wanted to buy a holiday home in Cork but didn't know where to start. We were referred to MyMortgages.ie (who specialise in arranging mortgages for Irish citizens living abroad) by a friend who recommended their services. We managed to secure a mortgage to buy a house in Ireland. The process was very smooth, and we felt that we were in trusted hands every step of the way. We would highly recommend MyMortgages.ie for Irish citizens living overseas.'

Paul Hanley

'I found that the experience was amazing for me. The service was fantastic. For me it was a switcher mortgage. I had been with my previous lender for a few years and like with all the other utilities, I hadn't investigated going with somebody different. When I rang MyMortgages.ie, the help I got was second-to-none in terms of preparing to present myself to the banks and I ended up making a saving of €400 a month and that's what I'm still saving at the moment compared to if I had stayed with my previous lender.'

Tara MacSweeney

'From start to finish I found Joey and all the staff at MyMortgages.ie to be absolutely excellent. No problem was too big or too small. They helped us with every bit of the transaction, right up to getting our keys and walking in the front door.'

Jody Cantillon

'[I found MyMortgages.ie to be] really, really good, I have to say. Particularly logging in through the website, getting the pack downloaded, they were really efficient from that point of view. Fantastic expertise from Joey as well, getting direction on how much to ask for, where you're going, the correct interest rate, term of loan. So, I really found it fantastic.'

John Fuller

'Taking out a mortgage, particularly for the first time, is one of the most significant decisions and one of the greatest financial commitments that most people take on in their lifetime. It is an extremely stressful process, with many essential steps along the way. There is little room for error, particularly in the current Irish banking environment, and so, being fully informed about all that needs to be done before one successfully obtains the key of the house is essential. However, it is not straightforward. In *The Mortgage Coach*, Joey Sheahan, in a very methodical and understandable manner, takes anybody considering taking out a mortgage to purchase a house through the whole process, including the preparation that needs to be done, the legal process, the engineer's report and snag list, and much more besides, before one successfully progresses to the end of the process. It is vital to avoid mistakes that could prove fateful, and in this regard, *The Mortgage Coach* will prove an invaluable ally.

'For anybody taking out a mortgage, particularly for the first time, I would strongly recommend this book. From a cost-benefit perspective, the time invested in reading this book and the monetary cost would be far outweighed by the benefits. In today's Ireland, taking out a mortgage is a very complicated process and to quote another Corkonian, "fail to prepare, prepare to fail". Joey Sheahan clearly has a deep understanding of the mortgage market and the mortgage process and, most importantly, can deliver the message in a very user-friendly manner, without the use of the type of jargon that is so commonplace amongst many practitioners in this market. For anybody interested in understanding the mortgage market, this book will make for very useful reading.'

Jim Power, Economist

'Joey Sheahan has written a must-read guide, relevant to anyone considering their first or long-term mortgage position. The content is insightful and practical, and it is evident that, like any great coach, he aims to focus the reader on taking the best steps to achieve a successful result!'

Michael McGrath TD, Fianna Fáil
Spokesperson on Finance

'Joey Sheahan's *The Mortgage Coach* is an invaluable guide through the mortgage maze. It takes a complex subject and breaks it down and simplifies it. The book is a must-read for anyone buying a home for the first time, building their own home, moving, switching mortgage, or acquiring a buy-to-let property.'

Charlie Weston, Personal Finance Editor, *Irish Independent*

'An easy-to-read, practical guide which will help everyone, irrespective of their mortgage stage in life. Mortgages are typically a product people only buy once or twice in their lifetime, and it can be a minefield with ever-changing rules. Joey easily cuts through the process, streamlining it, and makes it a far less daunting journey.'

Sinéad Ryan, Personal Finance Expert,
Journalist and Broadcaster

'It is important that we continue to remind ourselves that many of the mistakes made in causing Ireland's financial crisis were caused by bad decisions based upon poor information and advice, all of which, only too often, served the needs of lenders over those of borrowers. Many changes have been made to improve our financial institutions since then. However, one thing that has not changed is the continued desire of people living in Ireland to affordably and sustainably buy a home of their own. Getting the best choice of mortgage is the biggest financial decision that most of us will make in our lifetime. Having the right information and advice in preparing for that decision is of the greatest importance. This is why I believe *The Mortgage Coach* is a "must-read" for any person or couple planning to buy a home. The book is not just an invaluable resource for anyone considering a first-time mortgage, but is also a very useful asset for anyone seeking to review their existing mortgage or looking to see how they might reduce the costs of their monthly repayments.'

Ciarán Lynch, former TD and Chairperson of
the Oireachtas Joint Committee of Inquiry
into the Banking Crisis

DISCLAIMER

The content of this book does not address the circumstances of any particular individual or entity. Calculations on examples provided have been rounded to the nearest euro. The ideas and strategies should never be used without first assessing your own personal and financial situation, or without consulting an authorised mortgage broker. You alone assume the sole responsibility of evaluating the merits and risks associated with the use of any information or other content in the book before making any decisions based on such information or other content. The author does not allow for a guarantee of success and shall not be held liable for any possible claim for damages arising from any decision you make based on information or other content made available to you through the book. The opinions expressed in the text belong solely to the author.

As a resource to you, this book provides details of services and websites operated by third parties. Because the author has no control over such sites or their content, he is not responsible for the availability of such external sites or their content, and does not adopt, endorse, nor is he responsible or liable for any such sites or content, including advertising, products or other materials, on or available through such sites or resources. While care has been taken to ensure that information contained in this book is correct at the time of publication, changes in law and regulatory requirements after the time of publication may impact on the accuracy of this information.

PREFACE

In Ireland we share a rich history and culture that instills a natural aspiration in every man, woman and child for home ownership. In 2016, according to the CSO Census report profiling housing in Ireland, 67.6% of us continue to live in a home that we own. Changing attitudes in a changing Ireland and periods of economic uncertainty made us more open to alternatives, but the desire to have an affordable home providing comfort and security for our loved ones continues to be an abiding motivator in contemporary Ireland.

This book was written for all of those considering first entry into or a move within the property market. It serves as a practical, no-nonsense guide for first-time buyers and homeowners trading up, as well as those looking to downsize, and all mortgage holders who wish to explore how switching could benefit them.

By reading this book you will come to understand how the market works, and also gain insight into how important it is to prepare well and what to look for when determining your options in the long term. The step-by-step approach has been formed over twenty years of direct experience working with clients who faced real-life challenges in their mortgage journeys. This book provides the benefit of their stories, combined with expert knowledge to help you achieve the goal of your dream home.

I

MORTGAGE
PREPARATION

CHAPTER 1

FIRST STEPS FOR FIRST-TIME BUYERS

In the Beginning ...

You're renting an apartment with college friends and are in the early years of your career. Or you're still living with your parents while you build up your savings for a deposit. Now that your job is more secure and you see a steady path ahead of you, it seems like the right time to think about getting the keys to your own place. However, whether you're considering buying an apartment with a friend or sibling, or taking the big step of moving in with your partner, remember, a mortgage is the biggest financial undertaking most of us will ever make in our lifetime.

The word 'mortgage' translates from the French as 'death pledge', and while this may make it sound daunting, it doesn't have to be. If you arm yourself with a detailed knowledge of the process, you will be prepared for the road ahead and will therefore be able to easily navigate the twists and turns in order to arrive at your destination – your new home.

But before you start down this road, you need to be utterly sure that it's the right route for you.

Considerations before you start

How you arrive at this decision will be based on a myriad of factors:

- Timing: Is it the right time for you?
- Deposit: Can I save a 10% deposit, plus the associated costs such as 1% stamp duty and say another 1% towards fees?
- Monthly costs: How much rent am I paying monthly now? In contrast, how much would a mortgage cost me on a monthly basis? Engage an expert to run the mortgage calculations for you. This will give you a good indication of whether or not buying makes financial sense in your current situation.

With the last two points in particular, it basically boils down to affordability. This is the key consideration. You need to consider your potential mortgage repayments and your ability to save enough for a deposit to meet the Central Bank's mortgage lending rules (also known as 'measures') for determining whether or not you can secure a mortgage.

These rules were introduced in 2015 and are reviewed each year. Their purpose is to ensure that buyers cannot borrow more than they can afford to repay, and that banks and lending institutions are prudent in how they lend money. The rules basically serve to determine the amount of money that can be borrowed to buy residential property; this is done using loan-to-value (LTV) limits and loan-to-income (LTI) limits. First-time buyers, for example, can obtain a loan for 90% of the value of their house and up to 3.5 times their annual gross income (i.e. before tax is deducted), though in some instances stronger applicants can be entitled to more than 3.5 times. (I will delve into these requirements in more detail in Chapter 3.)

Let's look at an example:

Kerrie and Rory go to buy a house in Dundrum. Each of them has an annual gross basic salary of €40,000. They want to purchase a house for €300,000 and they're looking to borrow 90% of this, which is a €270,000 loan amount. Multiplying their combined income by 3.5 we get a total of €280,000, so the €270,000 loan required is within Central Bank limits.

Their monthly repayments over thirty-five years would be €1,062 based on a variable interest rate of 3.15%. The cost of the mortgage in this scenario is likely to be much lower than the rent for a similar property in Dundrum. So, based on these calculations, it makes financial sense for Kerrie and Rory to give a house purchase serious consideration as soon as they can get a deposit together and decide on their preferred location.

Mortgage	Term	Variable Interest Rate	Monthly Payment	Total Interest
€270,000	35	3.15%	€1,062	€175,968

However, they will need to factor in ancillary costs associated with taking out a mortgage, including survey expenses, stamp duty, moving costs and legal fees. Additional expenses also include mortgage protection and home insurance – these are usually mandatory under the conditions of the bank's mortgage loan offer. Still, even taking these into consideration, the house purchase would likely still make sense for Kerrie and Rory in this case.

Finding your Dream Home

Once you have made your decision to buy, that's when the real fun begins! Finding a property and securing a mortgage can be done at the same time, but it is advisable to have some of the legwork on the mortgage application done in advance of property hunting. (See Chapter 2 for more information on how to prepare.) For example, most estate agents/ auctioneers will not accept a bid unless you can show them a copy of your 'approval in principle'. This is a document that a lender will provide, stating their approval of a mortgage for you up to a certain amount based on the details you have given in your application. A mortgage approval in principle will usually be valid for six months.

When looking for a property, it is important to ask yourself:

- What type of property am I looking for? Would I consider an apartment? Do I need a minimum number of bedrooms? Would I like a garden? Do I require parking spaces? What about other specific requirements?

- Where would I like to live? Your level of flexibility in this regard will determine how much choice you have. Start with your ideal location and work your way from there. You could list the pros and cons of each location to get a clearer picture.

- Is your place of employment a deal-breaker? For many people proximity to their workplace will be one of the primary considerations in choosing a property. But, depending on how long you intend to stay in the property, you should also consider other factors. Do you want to live close to family members? Or friends? Is access to transportation important? What amenities are nearby, e.g. schools, parks, childcare and community facilities, sports clubs, shopping centre, coastline?

And, of course, you must once again consider:

- How much can I afford to spend?
- How much do I want to repay on a monthly basis?

The next step is homework!

Talk to local estate agents and browse property websites such as daft.ie or myhome.ie to get an idea of what's out there and current market prices. Line up some viewings.

If you are considering moving close to friends or family, ask them about their neighbourhood; they will give you a better sense of the area than a property website will – for example, whether it's a bottleneck for traffic that restricts movement and access, or if there are ongoing problems with contaminated water, sewage treatment or fly-tipping.

It's also a good idea to visit the area of a property you are interested in at different times of the day and night before making a bid, in order to see if there is a problem with anti-social behaviour, disturbances, etc., in the area.

Even if you are not ready to make a bid on a house just yet, getting a 'feel' for what you are looking for and what's out there is the first step in the process towards moving into your new home.

When deciding to buy, particularly if you are going to buy in a new development, off the plans, there are some other elements to watch out for. Such as, what if your neighbours are student renters and party all night? If you're also a student you may not mind, but you will if you have a sleeping baby!

It's important to keep all this in mind when beginning the process of applying for your mortgage.

CHAPTER 2

PREPARING FOR YOUR MORTGAGE APPLICATION

A mortgage is a huge undertaking and a process that needs to start months before you look at application forms. You might only get one bite of the cherry with a lender, after all, so it's crucial that you put your best foot forward. Otherwise they may not be willing to approve you for six to twelve months.

Fail to Prepare, Prepare to Fail

Saving a deposit for a mortgage is generally the first step of the process. The length of time will vary from person to person. While one applicant may have to save for a few years depending on their available surplus income, another person might be fortunate enough to receive a gift of some or all of the deposit from a parent or via an inheritance.

However, deposit aside, if you're considering taking your first steps onto the property ladder, you should begin the preparatory work at least three, but ideally six, months before submitting your application to any potential lender. Preparation is key to success. And as you begin your preparation, it is important to keep in mind what factors a lender will take into account when considering your application.

Red Flags and your Credit Rating

Before considering a mortgage application, a lender will first look at the applicant's credit history and recent banking history. Ultimately, what they are looking for is proven capacity to repay any loan given and a tendency to meet financial obligations as evidenced by past behaviour. There are a number of 'red flags' that will put a lender off, so applicants must ensure that these are not raised on their application:

- Overdrafts: Applicants must operate within the limit of their overdraft.
- Online gambling referred to on your bank or credit card statements, or even the use of pre-paid charge cards for gambling, can be an issue. Have supporting documentation for any regular payments.
- Cash advances on credit cards, even for holidays, can be an issue.
- Non-documentation of regular payments such as rent.
- An irregular savings pattern – banks prefer this to be consistent and regular.
- Erratic spending.
- A poor credit history.
- Referral charges or unpaid direct debit charges on your current account.

– Over-limit charges on credit cards.

Steps to Success

I recommend taking the following steps in the months before applying to boost your chances of success:

Rent: Ensure your monthly payment is paid through your bank account rather than in cash, as lenders will usually not accept rent paid as proven repayment ability unless it is evidenced on your bank statement.

Overdrafts: Even if you have an approved overdraft facility, it is better not to use it on a regular basis. If you do, aim to clear it and leave it that way for at least six months before approaching your bank.

Credit cards: Avoid using credit to pay for everyday expenses. Regular use of credit cards and cash advances from credit cards in particular can indicate poor money-management habits. However, if you do need a credit card, ensure that balances are cleared each month or at least that the minimum monthly payment is met each month. Aside from this portraying a better picture of the applicant, it will also save you a considerable sum on interest – some credit card companies charge up to 18% APR on outstanding balances.

Credit rating report: You can request this free of charge, from either the Central Credit Register (CCR) or the Irish Credit Bureau (ICB). (See Chapter 4 for more details.)

Outstanding loans: These include personal contract plans, personal loans, car loans, etc. – keep monthly repayments up to date. Arrears are a no-no. It's the monthly repayment amount rather than the loan balance outstanding that will affect how much you can borrow. Sometimes it's worth considering consolidating a number of loans into one loan with one monthly payment.

Savings: Transfer your savings into one dedicated account and save a regular amount each month. Avoid making withdrawals from this dedicated savings account. It's better to save less on a monthly basis and then add extra when you can, rather than over-saving and then dipping into your savings account.

Deposit: Getting a deposit together can take years. And while you do not need to have all of your deposit before you apply, you can get 'approval in principle' when the lender can see that you have the required percentage of the purchase price available. Typically, this is 10% for a first-time buyer; 20% of the purchase price for a non-first-time buyer and 30% of the purchase price for a buy-to-let investor. In addition, a borrower will also need to show that they have sufficient funds available to cover additional costs such as stamp duty and professional fees, which could be approximately 2% of the purchase price in total. A gift letter confirming that the deposit amount is available will suffice for the application stage.

Employment: Permanent employees have an advantage. But applicants are reviewed on a case-by-case basis. Self-employed applicants should ensure their accounts are up to date and that all relevant returns have been filed with Revenue. Contract workers should include a copy of their CV as well as their last three P60s or tax balancing statements and their last two or three contracts.

Joint or single borrower: Banks still often favour joint borrowers over a single applicant because there is less risk. The way they see it, if one applicant loses their job and is unable to keep up the repayments, the other might have the financial means to do so. So it could be worth considering taking out a joint mortgage, maybe with a family member, for example.

Age: It's not something that you have any control over, of course, but if you are planning ahead into your retirement, it's useful to bear in mind that banks do factor the applicant's age into the approval decision. Lenders prefer applicants who have a long way to go to retirement age as the mortgage can be stress tested over a longer period, meaning the younger you are the more you can borrow. The maximum age for borrowers at the end of the mortgage repayment term is currently seventy, or seventy-five for buy-to-let investors. Some lenders may support borrowers into their retirement based on evidence of affordability.

The Mortgage Application Checklist

Once you have dealt with the potential red flags, it will be time to start on your application. Each lender has its own application form and information criteria, but generally you will need the following:

- Photo identification.
- Proof of address.
- Marriage certificate (if relevant).
- Certificate of income – to be completed and stamped by employer.
- P60 or tax balancing statement for previous year.
- Payslips – three if paid monthly, six if fortnightly, thirteen if weekly.
- Current account statements – previous six months.
- Savings account statements – previous six months.
- Credit card statements – previous six months.
- Loan and/or mortgage statements – previous twelve months.
- Copy of credit history. (See more in Chapter 4.)

Note: Self-employed applicants require additional paperwork. Have a look at Chapter 5 for more information.

Taking the Next Step: the Mortgage Application

This part of the process can take anywhere from two weeks to six months or more, depending on how 'mortgage ready' you are to begin with.

You have two options:

- Approach each lender directly yourself – in which case

they will advise you of the preparation work, forms to fill out, and how the application process works, or

- Choose a mortgage broker, authorised by the Central Bank of Ireland, who can approach a number of lenders on your behalf – again they will advise you on what you need to do to put forward the 'perfect' mortgage application. Each bank has its own criteria, so it's often worth having some 'inside knowledge' on how best to present your application and how to approach each lender. Furthermore, credit policies vary between banks. Different lenders will approve different amounts for the same application, so a mortgage broker will know which bank will approve what and at the best rates – thus saving you a lot of time.

Whichever route you choose, be aware that the mortgage application process can be a long one, so getting your application right first time round will save you the trouble of having to go through the whole process again … and again.

Furthermore, one bank may approve an application while another may decline the same application. This is down to each bank's own credit policy. For example, some banks won't approve a teacher who is not permanent, whereas other banks will, once they can show that they have been working consistently for a few years.

Success! I've secured Mortgage Approval – now what?

Once you have received your approval in principle letter, you should speak with your broker or lender. At this stage you will:

- Decide on the term of your mortgage. You may be given an option of a twenty-five, thirty or thirty-five-year term, or you may simply be given just one choice, depending on your age.

Banks will lend up to a maximum age of seventy, so an applicant who is thirty-five or younger can choose a term of up to thirty-five years. An applicant who is fifty can only choose a term of up to twenty years. Because the fifty-year-old is repaying the loan over a shorter period, the bank would use a shorter term to stress test their ability to repay than it would with a thirty-five-year-old applicant, which may reduce the amount the older applicant qualifies for.

- Decide on whether your rate will be fixed or variable – this decision should be given careful consideration.

A variable rate is an interest rate that can rise or fall depending on a variety of factors – most fluctuate as the banks' cost of funds fluctuate and/or as the European Central Bank rates change, though they are not directly tied to the ECB rates. There are several types of variable rates, but the most common is the standard variable rate (SVR). Each bank has autonomy to vary this rate at any time as they see fit.

In contrast, a fixed rate is an interest rate that is set for a specific period – sometimes three, five or even ten years. Over the term agreed, the rate cannot change.

When deciding which rate to choose the following question grid might give you some guidance:

Question	Yes	No
Do I favour certainty over all else?	Fixed	Variable
Do I have financial capacity to handle any changes in interest rates?	Variable	Fixed
Do I want the flexibility to overpay the monthly mortgage repayment amount?	Variable	Fixed*
Am I willing to pay extra for a sense of security in relation to monthly outgoings?	Fixed	Variable
Is there a likelihood that my monthly income will vary?	Variable	Fixed
Am I good at budgeting and managing my finances?	Variable	Fixed

Note: this question grid is a very simplified general guide which you can use to start your 'fixed versus variable' conversation.

* Some banks will allow overpayment with no penalty while on a fixed rate.

Entering a long-term fixed rate can be risky, as interest rates may fall; however, there is arguably more risk with a shorter-term fixed rate as interest rates fluctuate and may have risen considerably by the time you are exiting a fixed rate. For example, if a borrower takes a mortgage over a twenty-five-year term and they opt for a fixed rate for the first ten years, then they are only vulnerable to interest rate fluctuations for the final fifteen years, whereas if the same borrower opts for a fixed rate for the first three years, then they are leaving themselves vulnerable to interest rate fluctuations for the final twenty-two years. So, we can see that taking a longer fixed rate term gives more certainty in monthly mortgage repayments.

Your decision will depend on your individual situation, of course. Consider whether you think you might be able to increase your monthly payments or pay a lump sum off your mortgage over the next ten years. There may be an early breakage fee with some lenders, but others allow you to make additional lump sum repayments towards your mortgage without any such fee. This varies from lender to lender and should be outlined in your letter of loan offer. (See more about overpayments in Chapter 13.)

Ultimately, a fixed rate will give you the peace of mind of knowing exactly what you will pay over a specific period and help you to budget accordingly. For some people this certainty is invaluable. Other mortgage holders may prefer to avail of lower rates now in the expectation that their income will rise over time. So, it's important to consider your options here and the implications.

You should seek expert advice on this decision. Taking on a mortgage is likely to be your biggest monthly expenditure, so any decisions you make around it should be carefully considered.

Here's an example:

Sisters Mary and Anne both work full-time. Mary has just qualified as an accountant, and earns €35,000 per annum working for an international accountancy firm. She expects her income to increase each year and is aware that some of her peers who have been with the company for five years are earning €55,000. Anne, on the other hand, is a self-employed music teacher, currently earning €35,000 per annum. Anne's income is not guaranteed and is just as likely to decrease in the future as to increase. As such, it would be more prudent for Anne to opt for a fixed interest rate, so she can be certain of her mortgage outgoings for a number of years. Mary, on the other hand, has the luxury of choosing a variable rate or a fixed rate, as her income in the future is almost certain to increase, which leaves her less vulnerable to future interest rate fluctuations.

Best of Both Worlds

It should be stressed that most – though not all – banks will allow you to split your rate, meaning you can opt to fix a portion as well as leave a portion on a variable rate.

For example, a borrower is borrowing €300,000. They can decide how much they wish to fix and how much to leave on a variable rate. So, they could choose to fix €200,000 with €100,000 on a variable rate, or to have €150,000 fixed with €150,000 on a variable rate.

Amid the mortgage-acquiring process, whether it be fixed rates or letters of approval or credit rating reports, it is essential that you have a strong understanding of the Central Bank's criteria for mortgage applicants.

CHAPTER 3

CENTRAL BANK CRITERIA
AND EXEMPTIONS

Note: While care has been taken to ensure that information contained in this book is correct at the time of publication, changes in Central Bank of Ireland rules after the time of publication may impact on the accuracy of this information.

The Rules

The Central Bank of Ireland introduced new rules around mortgage lending in February 2015, which have since been amended. The measures were put in place to prevent the reoccurrence of a property bubble by restricting the way banks and other lenders issued home loans. The rules also limit the amount that mortgage applicants can borrow to avoid excess credit building up within the Irish financial system.[1]

Essentially, the rules limit how much a bank can lend to a mortgage seeker based on two factors: the deposit required in relation to the property's value (loan-to-value – LTV)

---

1   https://www.centralbank.ie/consumer-hub/explainers/what-are-the-mortgage-measures.

and the applicant's income compared to the loan (loan-to-income – LTI).

The rules can vary depending on what type of buyer category you fit into (e.g. first-time, second-time or subsequent, buy-to-let). The rules dictate the ceiling limits for each category of how much you can borrow and how much the banks can lend to you, as well as the minimum deposit amount that you are required to have in place in order to secure a mortgage from a bank. Self-build applications are also subject to slightly different limits. The CBI reviews these rules on an annual basis.

All mortgage applicants need to understand how the lending rules apply to them, so that they can calculate how much of a deposit they will need and the value of the mortgage they might be eligible for.

How is the LTI calculated?

Your income will determine the maximum mortgage you can apply for – and lenders will look at how you earn this income. While there can be some exceptions to the rules, in general most banks have the following requirements:

- Applicants must be in permanent or 'sustainable' employment.
- If you are a PAYE worker, a lender will look at who your employer is and what type of work contract you have.
- If you are self-employed, a lender will usually look to

ensure you have been trading for a minimum of two years.

- Contract workers or those in temporary employment might find it more difficult to get mortgage approval. But there can be ways around this – it's best to seek expert advice in this case.

The income figure used when calculating the LTI is the applicant's gross annual salary (before tax). In the case of joint applicants, incomes are combined. So, for example, a couple with a combined annual gross income of €100,000 can borrow up to €350,000.

What constitutes as income can vary slightly from one lender to another – but the applicant's basic salary is the primary consideration. Some lenders will include all or a portion of additional income such as car allowance, bonuses, overtime, shift allowance, commission, etc., and will allow you to borrow 3.5 times the higher income amount.

Let's look at the following examples:

Elizabeth and Ken want to buy a house in Malahide. Each has an annual gross basic salary of €35,000. The house is for sale for €300,000. They want to borrow 90% of this, which would mean a €270,000 loan amount. It is unlikely they will qualify for this loan amount, as 3.5 times their combined income is €245,000. They will probably not get an exemption (see pp. 44–5) at this level of income.

However, lenders tend to favour applicants with higher earning power.

Let's look at the case of newly-weds Adele and John, who are both aged thirty-five. The couple are both fully qualified solicitors, earning €65,000 per annum each. They want to buy a house for €600,000 and are hoping to borrow 90%, which is €540,000. There is a very strong chance that they will qualify for an exemption of €540,000, which is over four times their income, as their combined income is very strong, and they are both professionals whose income is likely to increase as they progress in their careers.

How is the LTV calculated?

The deposit you need will be determined by the price of your property and the type of buyer you are. First-time buyers can borrow up to 90% of property value. Second-time and subsequent buyers can borrow 80% of the property value only.

While you may not have settled on a particular property at the time of applying for a mortgage, you will need to first calculate your LTI limit – 3.5 times your salary – to ascertain your maximum loan eligibility.

Take Mark as an example. He is earning a basic salary of €60,000. Once he meets all of the lender's credit policy criteria, he should be able to borrow €210,000, this being 3.5 times his annual gross salary (i.e. before tax). He also earns an annual bonus of €5,000. Some banks may include a portion or all of this amount, which would increase the €210,000. Mark may also qualify for a LTI exemption, meaning he could borrow more than 3.5 times his income; however, this will be at the discretion of the bank he is applying to. Lenders are allowed to grant loans in excess of 3.5 times income, up to 20% of the value of mortgages to first-time buyers and 10% of the value of mortgages to non-first-time buyers.

Next, you should find out how much you can get for a deposit, as this will allow you to determine how much you can apply for. If a first-time buyer wants to purchase a property for €300,000, for example, but they only have a deposit of €25,000 available, then they will not be able to purchase this property as they are required to have at least a 10% deposit, which is €30,000. In this instance, a purchase price of €200,000 would be more realistic as the €25,000 deposit available should cover the 10% deposit of €20,000 as well as associated costs including stamp duty and professional fees, which would be, approximately, an additional 2% of the purchase price.

Table 1 | Details of the LTV and the LTI Regulations, 2019

LTV Limits	For primary dwelling home (PDHs):	First-time buyers (FTBs): 90%	5% of new lending to FTBs allowed above 90%
		Non-FTBs: 80%	20% of non-FTB new lending allowed above 80%
	For buy-to-let borrowers (BTLs):	70% LTV limit	10% of new lending allowed above the BTL limit
LTI Limit	For PDHs:	3.5 times income	20% of new lending to FTBs allowed above 3.5 limit
			10% of non-FTB new lending allowed above 3.5 limit
Exemptions	**From LTV limit:**	**From LTI limit:**	**From both limits:**
	Borrowers in negative equity	BTL borrowers	Switcher mortgages
			Restructuring of mortgages in arrears

Table explaining the LTV and LTI regulations. Reproduced with kind permission of the Central Bank of Ireland.[2]

---

2 Central Bank of Ireland, 'Review of residential mortgage requirements: Mortgage Measures 2018', available to download from https://www.centralbank.ie/financial-system/financial-stability/macro-prudential-policy/mortgage-measures.

Mortgage Rule Exemptions

Exemptions are available to some applicants who fall outside the LTV or LTI limits. However, there is a strict quota imposed on lenders as to how many mortgages they can approve under these exemptions. For this reason, the annual quota can be used up early in a year when the demand from mortgage applicants is high.

		FTBs	Non-FTBs
LTV Limits	Primary Dwelling Homes	90%	80%
	Self-Build		
LTV Limits	Primary Dwelling Homes	3.5 times income	3.5 times income
	Self-Build		
Exemptions	LTV	5% of new lending allowed above 90% LTV	20% of new lending above 80% LTV limit
	LTI	20% of new lending allowed above 3.5 LTI	10% of new lending above 3.5 LTI limit

You can get an exemption under only one of the lending rules, LTV or LTI.

Each lender grants exemptions at its own discretion. For

example, one bank may require a minimum €40,000 income for a sole applicant and €70,000 income for a couple to be considered for an exemption. Other criteria, such as your proven repayment capacity, credit history, job security, etc., will also be considered. Each exemption application is considered on a case-by-case basis. (See more on exemptions in Chapter 10.)

Know your Limits

- Examine the mortgage lending rules above and assess how they apply to you.
- Figure out how much you will be eligible to borrow in order to ascertain which properties are in your price range. (Note – the amount you *can* borrow is not a target and is not necessarily the same as the amount you *should* borrow. Getting into more debt than you need is never a good idea. So, think about the amount you would feel comfortable repaying.)
- Decide if you need to apply for an exemption and seek advice on what would be your best chance of success in this case.

Taking the time to consider and understand the rules and limits at the earliest stage of the process makes sense. With the facts in hand, you will be able to focus on all of the 'right-size' property options in the market that suit your needs.

CHAPTER 4

YOUR CREDIT RATING

What is my Credit History and Rating?

Your credit history gives a more detailed and comprehensive picture of your credit behaviour – in other words, it measures your repayment of all loans. Your 'performance' as a borrower is then given a rating.

A lender will look to this rating as evidence of your ability and willingness to repay loans given to you. Potential creditors see this history as an indication of future behaviour. The higher your rating, the better. However, the main point is that you have not had any late or missed payments within the past five years.

Let's look at an example:

John was living and working in Australia from 2009 to 2018. While he was away, he was earning very good money and managed to save a significant deposit of €100,000. He is now back living and working in Ireland and earning €50,000 as a carpenter. However, he has run into an issue. He had a credit card before he emigrated, and he forgot to close the account when he moved abroad. Unknown to him, the government levy was charged to his card while he was away, and the card was revoked. He eventually became aware of the issue in 2017 and he cleared the card and closed the account in full in December 2017. This oversight has affected John's credit rating. Generally, your credit rating history is held for five years and because of this most banks won't offer a mortgage to John for five years from when he closed the credit facility, which would bring him up to December 2022. However, some lenders will lend to John on a case-by-case basis, once his credit issue has been resolved for more than two years. So, in this case, John is fortunate, and he may have options sooner than expected.

How do I find out?

Before applying for a mortgage, it's advisable to check your credit rating. You can do this free of charge. You may have loans in the past that you missed a payment on – knowledge is power here – so it's best to get the full facts before approaching your bank. If there are discrepancies, you can try to fix them or work out an explanation of your case to a potential lender.

You can request your credit rating, free of charge, from either the Central Credit Register (CCR) or the Irish Credit Bureau (ICB).

The CCR was set up in 2017 and runs parallel to the ICB, which has been in operation since 1963. Both entities hold information of a borrower's credit history – as provided to them by lending institutions.

Your credit history and rating will be affected by the following:

- The number of loans you have had.
- The frequency with which you have applied for and taken out loans.
- Whether or not you missed any payments.
- Whether or not you were late with repayments.
- Whether or not you paid off the loan within the agreed time frame.

There are instances where a lender may have reported incorrect information to a credit rating agency in error. In such circumstances, the lender is obliged to correct same.

Keep it High

A person's credit rating is determined by their own behaviour. There are a number of 'best practices' that you can adopt to establish and keep a high credit rating:

- Keep up with loan repayments. When you take out any form of credit you enter into an agreement with a lender that sets out exactly when and how much you agree to pay off over a set period. Do not miss payments. Repay in full the amount that has been agreed within the time agreed. If you are paying a loan by direct debit, then you must ensure that you have sufficient funds in your account to cover the cost of the repayment each month.

- Less is more when it comes to taking out credit. It stands to reason that the more lines of credit you have, the harder they will be to manage and keep track of.

- If you do fall into arrears on a loan, take action immediately. Pick up the phone and call your lender to explain the situation. If affordability is an issue do not take a 'head in the sand' approach. Lenders have processes in place to work with borrowers who find themselves in financial difficulty.

- A minimum payment due on a credit card (usually 5% of the balance outstanding) – no matter how small – must be paid on time and in full. It is not acceptable to pay nothing one month and extra the next to make up for the missed payment.

- Be mindful of where you are on overdraft and credit card limits. It can be easy to run over on these, particularly when you are away on holidays and may be spending more than usual. Spending outside the limits can lead to additional charges from your bank and possibly a poor credit rating.

I have a poor Credit Rating – am I doomed?

If you discover that there is an issue with your credit history, then do not despair – all may not be lost! While lenders do not look favourably on credit rating red flags, they will often be willing to listen to an applicant's side of the story. If you can convince them that the red flag in question was a one-off, or perhaps a misunderstanding, then you might still be in with a shot of mortgage approval.

If you have a broker, then you should ask them for advice on the best way to present your case to the lender. If not, then writing a letter to the lender, setting out the facts as you understand them and making your case in a logical and concise manner might be the best option. It will then be up to the bank to decide if they will look past the red flag.

Sometimes, however, a person's credit rating may simply be too low for any lender to consider their mortgage application. In this case you will have to take a step back and accept that you have some work to do to improve your rating before you can apply or reapply for a mortgage.

Be aware that this can take some time. For some lenders it's two years, for others more – but after five years all lenders should be willing to reconsider your application.

You should take expert advice if you find yourself in this position. There are specialist lenders on the market who cater for people with a poor or incomplete credit history. (See Chapter 17 for more details.)

Let's look at another example:

Patrick was previously married. When the marriage broke down, Patrick moved out of the family home. He was paying rent and also trying to contribute to the mortgage of the house where his wife and child continued to live. However, his outgoings were unsustainable and unfortunately Patrick fell into arrears on the mortgage.

The house was subsequently sold in May 2016 for an amount that just about cleared the mortgage in full. Since then, Patrick has not had any credit issues and has been paying rent, but now wants to buy a new home for himself. As his credit history is kept on record for five years, Patrick will have to wait until May 2021 for a clean bill of financial health. He should be able to qualify for a mortgage at that point, once he avoids any further credit issues in the interim. Some banks may consider lending to him sooner.

How can I fix it?

If you find yourself in a position where your credit rating is too low to have any hope of securing a mortgage right now, then it may be advisable to take some expert budgeting advice either from a financial advisor or from the Money Advice and Budgeting Service (MABS).

– From this point on, you need to 'stay on top' of your finances, which means having a clear picture of your monthly expenditure – what's coming in and what's going out – and stick to a budget.

- You should also contact your existing lenders to discuss your repayment schedule or restructuring of a loan agreement into something more manageable.

- Do not apply for any new lines of credit. The goal is to manage what you already have and to clear your loans as quickly as possible.

- Taking out a lower interest loan to clear a high interest credit card bill may make sense.

A specialist advisor should be able to offer advice in this area.

CHAPTER 5

OTHER CONSIDERATIONS WHEN GETTING MORTGAGE READY

There are some other avenues to consider and potentially avail of when applying for a mortgage. An analysis of some of these options follows.

The Help-to-Buy Scheme

This incentive is a scheme operated by the Revenue Commissioners for first-time buyers to help with the deposit needed to buy or build a new house or apartment. You must be buying or building the property to live in as your home. All applicants must be first-time buyers to avail of the scheme.

Subject to the Revenue Commissioners' criteria, the amount that you can claim is the lesser of:

- €20,000.
- 5% of the purchase price of a new home. For self-builds this is 5% of the completion value of the property.

To avail of this scheme:

- You must be borrowing a minimum of 70% of the value of the property.
- You must be tax compliant. If you are self-assessed, you must also have tax clearance.

Note: You can find more information about the scheme on the Revenue Commissioners' website.

Take the example of Sophie and Richie:

Sophie and Richie are both on a salary of €35,000 per annum. They want to buy a house similar in size to their rented accommodation in a new development in Galway for €270,000. The couple therefore need a total of around €32,000 to purchase the property, which is made up as follows: 10% or €27,000 deposit, plus 1% stamp duty of €2,700 and €2,300 towards legal costs.

They are currently paying rent of €1,300, so have only managed to save €5,000 for a deposit so far. However, their parents are each willing to gift the couple a total of €15,000. The house also qualifies for the Revenue's 'help-to-buy' scheme.[1] So Sophie and Richie can claim up to 5% of the purchase price of the house as a tax rebate, which is €13,500 in this example.

---

1 Applicants need to meet all of Revenue's criteria in order to qualify for the help-to-buy scheme.

Although the couple have a relatively small amount of savings, with the assistance of Revenue's help-to-buy scheme, as well as some family support, they are in a position to borrow €243,000 to purchase a property in their location of choice.

Mortgage repayment figures on €243,000 over thirty-five years at a ten-year fixed interest rate of 3.3% are €976 per month.

Mortgage	Term	Fixed 10-yr Interest Rate	Monthly Payment	Total Interest
€243,000	35	3.3%	€ 976	€167,064

Gift

Many first-time buyers receive cash gifts from their parents towards the deposit. While this doesn't impact on the criteria, lenders now require you to have a gift letter from the donor specifying the sum of money, the donor's name and signature, and confirmation that you do not need to repay the money and that the donor has no claim to the property.

It is important to keep in mind that there may be tax implications if you receive a cash gift from your parents towards your deposit. (Review the tax-free thresholds and exemptions under the inheritance and gifts rules on the Revenue website.)

Let's look at a couple of examples:

Amy is fortunate enough to have a grandmother who is willing to assist her with a deposit towards a purchase of a home. Some banks will allow Amy to receive all of her deposit as a gift, whereas others will require the mortgage applicant to have a minimum portion of the purchase price saved, typically around 5%.

Anyone can receive a gift of up to €3,000 annually, from anyone else without any tax implications.

So, to look at another example, George and Catherine are buying a house and their parents want to help them out with the deposit.

Catherine's mother gifts Catherine €3,000 in December 2020

Catherine's mother gifts George €3,000 in December 2020

Catherine's father gifts Catherine €3,000 in December 2020

Catherine's father gifts George €3,000 in December 2020

George's mother gifts Catherine €3,000 in December 2020

George's mother gifts George €3,000 in December 2020

George's father gifts Catherine €3,000 in December 2020

George's father gifts George €3,000 in December 2020

Catherine's mother gifts Catherine €3,000 in January 2021

Catherine's mother gifts George €3,000 in January 2021

Catherine's father gifts Catherine €3,000 in January 2021

Catherine's father gifts George €3,000 in January 2021

George's mother gifts Catherine €3,000 in January 2021

George's mother gifts George €3,000 in January 2021

George's father gifts Catherine €3,000 in January 2021

George's father gifts George €3,000 in January 2021

Total gifted with no tax liability within a two-month period is €48,000.

It is important to keep capital acquisitions tax thresholds in mind when receiving help with your deposit.

Buy-to-Let Mortgages

If you are buying a property to rent out to someone else, you can borrow up to 70% of the value of the property, meaning that you will need a minimum 30% deposit. Some banks assess an application for a buy-to-let property differently to a primary dwelling house application. The rent attainable from the property can be more relevant than an individual's personal income and a borrower can, depending on the bank, potentially be approved for a higher loan amount on a buy-to-let property than they might be on a primary dwelling house. It should be noted that most lenders require an applicant to already own a property before they will consider accepting an application for a buy-to-let property from them. The Central Bank will allow up to 10% of the value of mortgages issued by a lender to buy-to-let buyers to exceed 70%. (Go to Chapter 6 for more information on this.)

Other Associated Costs

It is important to remember these, because it can be easy to forget the critical need to factor in additional charges when your central focus is on funding the mortgage:

- Legal fees: Before you choose a solicitor, ask about their fees and other costs you have to pay, such as Land Registry and search fees. Fees could be around 1% but this will vary depending on the price of the property.

- Stamp duty: The amount is based on the value of a property. Stamp duty is currently charged at 1% of the value of the property up to €1,000,000 and 2% for anything over that. For example, if a property is valued at €1,250,000, then €1,000,000 is charged at 1% or €10,000. The remaining €250,000 is charged at 2% or €5,000. Therefore, total stamp duty to be paid is €15,000. Your solicitor will typically arrange the payment for you when they are closing the sale.

- Surveyor or engineer fees to complete an inspection of the house before you buy.

- Cost of appliances, furniture and other contents for your new home.

- Valuation fees are usually around €150–200. This pays for a professional valuer to give your lender an estimate of a property's market value. Some lenders cover the cost of the valuation. The valuation report is crucial in the process. When buying a house, buyers are entitled to borrow a percentage of the purchase price. However, in the event that the house is valued for an amount less than the purchase price, then the buyer is only entitled to borrow a percentage of the lower valuation amount or the market value.

For example, Bobby is a first-time buyer, bidding on a house in Dublin 4. Demand is strong among buyers and Bobby ends up in a bidding war. He purchases the property for €420,000 even though the guide price was €395,000. He subsequently arranges a valuation as is required by his bank and the property is valued at €410,000. Bobby is limited to borrowing 90% of €410,000 which is €369,000 despite paying €420,000 for the property. This means he will need a deposit of €19,000 extra, as the maximum mortgage amount available is €9,000 less, based on the lower valuation, and he will also need to fund the additional €10,000 (the difference between the purchase price of €420,000 and the value of €410,000) from his own savings.

- Mortgage protection and the necessary building insurance. Mortgage protection insurance is a life insurance policy that pays off your mortgage if you or your co-borrower die during the term of the mortgage and runs concurrently to your mortgage term. It's a requirement for all lenders, but you aren't obligated to buy the policy from your lender. I would usually see clients spending around €90 to €100 monthly, which may include an element of specified illness cover or income protection.

For example, take the case of Paul and Catherine who had been approved for a mortgage. One of the conditions they must satisfy prior to drawing down the funds is to assign a life policy to their lender. This means that a lender is the legal owner of the life policy and any pay-out under the policy for such time until the mortgage is redeemed, i.e. paid off in full, at which point the lender will release their interest in the policy. This is a standard requirement and the amount of cover and term of the life policy must be sufficient and in line with the terms of the loan. For example, Paul and Catherine are borrowing €400,000 over thirty years, so their policy must have €400,000 cover over thirty years also.

It is advisable to apply for and incept your life policy as early as possible in your mortgage journey so that you can avert any delays/potential issues. In the case of Paul and Catherine, Catherine was referred to a medical consultant to investigate a minor recurring ailment. However, she could not attain life cover until such time that she had the all-clear from the consultant. The waiting list was six months. It is prudent to secure life cover in advance of or concurrent with your mortgage application, thereby minimising the risk of not being able to meet the lender's condition of assigning a life policy.

Finding the Right Mortgage for You

You can apply for a mortgage either directly to various lenders or through a mortgage broker, who will deal with lenders on your behalf.

It pays to compare the current rates on offer – so don't rush to take the first offer. You may be able to save significant amounts of money by shopping around. Most lenders have special offers to encourage you to move your mortgage to them, for example, whether it be cashback, a contribution towards legal fees, or payment of valuation fees.

Cashback offers can be particularly attractive because they give you money in the short term. But a mortgage is a long-term contract so it pays to calculate what the mortgage will cost you overall.

For example, take a €300,000 mortgage over thirty-five years. One bank is offering a variable rate of 3.15% and another is offering 3.5%. Total interest paid is €195,520 and €220,746 respectively. So, 0.35% difference in the interest rate can mean €25,226 in additional interest! Some lenders will offer inducements (e.g. cashback offers) of say 2% of loan amount, which would be €6,000 in this example. However, while it is nice to receive a lump sum of €6,000 in the short term, the additional interest of €25,226 far outweighs the gain over the longer term.

It's essential that you keep this kind of thing in mind when considering your options. There are of course other issues to consider, like tax.

Tax Considerations
Local Property Tax
Since 2013 all residential property owners have to pay an annual property tax based on the market value of their property.

It is a self-assessment tax; you calculate the amount due based on your own estimate of your home's market value. Revenue provides guidance on how to value your property on its website.

Before you buy a property, you must obtain the local property tax identification number and valuation from the seller. You should also check that all returns and payments have been filed and are up to date.

Rent-a-Room Scheme
If you decide to rent a room in your new home, the income you receive may be exempt from tax. To be eligible, the income must not exceed €14,000. If it does exceed the

threshold, then you will be taxed on the total amount. Under the scheme this can only be claimed by individual taxpayers. You cannot claim if the room is being rented to a direct family member (child or civil partner) or an employee or employer. But you can rent to a student who needs accommodation for a period of one month or for a full term. The scheme also excludes short-term lets, which would be to guests rather than tenants who, for example, could be coming to you through an online accommodation booking site.

Let's take Brian and Billy, twin brothers from Cork who have both been working for one of the Big 4 accountancy firms in Dublin for the past two years. Their salaries are €45,000 each and they currently pay €550 rent each. They have managed to save €10,000 each over the past two years and have now decided to purchase a four-bedroomed property in a commuter town for €350,000. The property is in a new development and qualifies for Revenue's help-to-buy scheme through which they can claim back €17,500 (i.e. 5% of the purchase price) and they are taking a mortgage for €315,000. They will both live in the property and rent out two rooms for €550 each per month. Based on a loan amount of €315,000 over thirty-five years on a ten-year fixed rate of 3.3%, they will repay €1,265 monthly to their bank. The €1,100 monthly rent they will receive from the two extra bedrooms is tax-free as the total annual amount of €13,200 is less than Revenue's €14,000 limit under the rent-a-room scheme. This means that they have a net monthly outlay of just €165. This isn't a bad result considering the alternative, which was both of them paying €550 per month in rent. This is where buying versus renting makes sense, particularly where you are availing of Revenue's schemes or reliefs.

Mortgage	Term	Fixed 10-yr Interest Rate	Monthly Payment	Total Interest
€315,000	35	3.3%	€1,265	€216,564

Mortgage Interest

For buy-to-let, you can write the mortgage interest off against the income as an allowable expense, which reduces your income tax bill on rental profits. For example, if you receive rental income from a property of €15,000 annually and you make interest repayments on your mortgage of €8,000, then the taxable amount will be €7,000 (other expenses such as insurance, letting and management fees, repairs and maintenance, etc., are also deductible, which could further reduce the taxable amount).

Grants

If you are considering purchasing a home that needs substantial renovation, you should also research which grants you may be eligible for, as this could represent substantial savings on the overall cost of the work.

Energy Efficiency Grant

If you are upgrading your home to make it more energy efficient, then you should check if you're eligible for a grant from the Sustainable Energy Authority of Ireland (SEAI).

Grants are available for insulation, heat pump systems, heating control, solar water heating and solar electricity. There are conditions attached to these grants along with eligibility criteria. Check out the SEAI website for further information.

Grants for insulation and heating controls are available to owners of dwellings built and occupied before 2006. Homes built after this should have been constructed to the 2003 Building Regulations and should not need significant insulation upgrades. Grants for heat pump systems and solar water heating are available to owners of homes built and occupied before 2011.

You can apply for the grants through the SEAI site or by post. Alternatively, you can apply through an energy partner of SEAI – this is a contractor who is registered to carry out works under the programme and authorised by SEAI to submit grant applications on behalf of homeowners.

Upgrade and Adaptation Grants

Of course, your research should also extend to other grant

supports that might be available to you through your local authority, such as an individual domestic well grant, housing adaptation grant to support mobility and disability, or housing aid for older people. Conditions and eligibility criteria do apply in these cases also.

Now that you have explored the various considerations on tax efficiencies, incentives and potential grant support opportunities, it's time to look at the type of buyer category into which you may fit.

II

TYPES OF BUYERS/ MORTGAGES

CHAPTER 6

BUY-TO-LET

A section of the property market that has generated a lot of headlines in recent years is the buy-to-let market. While renting property can deliver a significant return on investment, in the form of a regular income, as well as a long-term capital gain or loss, entering into a landlord-tenant relationship can be fraught with complications. Therefore, if you're thinking of dipping your toe into this area of the market, take time to consider if you're ready to become a landlord.

Are you ready to become a Landlord?

Owning a rental property is a big commitment. Before you make the leap into landlord territory, take time to consider scenarios like the following:

- Do you want to deal directly with tenants or would you prefer to outsource these duties to an agent?
- Do you see the property as a long-term investment or do you intend to sell it as soon as the market rises? If this is a short-term investment, it's important that you factor in capital gains tax that will be due. (See 'Tax Considerations' later in this chapter for more detail on this.)

– Is this property the first in a larger investment strategy or do you want to leave your options open?

Typically, when you're looking for a home to live in, you weigh up factors such as proximity to workplaces, schools and local amenities, as well as outdoor space such as a garden or patio. However, when considering buying-to-let, other factors come into play. Location may not be a priority – but the return on your investment will be. Your aim should be to buy while the market is low, thereby getting the best rental price for a property for potential tenants.

While everyone wants to buy for the lowest price possible, this can prove difficult, particularly if you have your sights set on a particular location – for example, a four-bed detached house in Dublin 6. This type of location will always be desirable among prospective buyers, so it could prove more difficult to get good value there, particularly when compared to a less central location.

Your Ideal Tenant

Where and what you buy will depend on your ideal tenant. For instance, are you planning to rent to a family, to students or to professionals?

Try to think like a landlord. Who are your ideal tenants? Once you have decided, look for a property that will be easy to rent out. For example, if you want to rent to students, luxury apartments far from colleges will not be appealing.

Similarly, a couple with a young family will want to be close to schools and likely prefer a low-maintenance garden.

There are of course other aspects for you to consider, such as: would you like it to be close to where you live so you can manage it or would you prefer it to be far away from your own community? Would you like it in a high-demand area where the rental income will be greater? Close to transport links and local amenities? Do you require a property that's ready to let or would you consider a house that needs renovation? Do you want a long-term let or do you plan to use the property as a holiday letting?

Do your Sums

- Write your own list, including your top priorities in terms of location, size or type of property and what type of tenant you want.

- Research the local market carefully – look at estate agent advertisements in conjunction with the Property Price Register, which lists what properties *actually* sold for.[1]

- Look at property websites to see what current market rents are for similar properties in your preferred area.

- Factor in one-off and recurring costs such as stamp duty, letting fees, maintenance, service charges and insurance.

- Work out the projected tax due on rental income. Allow for expenses, which can be written off against rental

1 Property Price Register, https://www.propertypriceregister.ie/website/npsra/pprweb.nsf/PPR?OpenForm.

income. (See 'Tax Considerations' section at the end of this chapter.)

Consider the case of Danny, who wants to buy a second property as a retirement investment.

Danny is an IT consultant living in Cork and is forty-five years of age. He has managed to accumulate savings of €100,000 over his working life. He is now planning for retirement and, as part of his portfolio, he wants to purchase an apartment near University College Cork that he will let out to either professionals or students.

The purchase price of apartments in the area he is looking at is approximately €250,000. He wants to borrow 70% or €175,000 and he will use his savings for the remainder. He hopes to let out the apartment for around €1,300 per month. This rent should support repayments to the level of €175,000 as the amount a bank will lend against a buy-to-let property is quite often based on the income from the property as well as on personal income.

Repayments on €175,000 over twenty-five years at a variable interest rate of 3.95% are €918 per month. Furthermore, all of the interest payable can be offset as an expense against the rental income, thereby reducing Danny's tax obligations.

Mortgage	Term	Variable Interest Rate	Monthly Payment	Total Interest
€ 175,000	25	3.95%	€918	€ 100,667

Factor in Initial Costs

It is imperative that you factor in initial costs. These include:

- **Survey costs:** Costs vary according to the type of survey. Don't skip this if you want to avoid costly structural problems down the line.
- **Legal fees:** Both parties to a property transaction – buyer and vendor – need to hire a solicitor to carry out legal paperwork.
- **Property valuation:** This is charged by the lender. Some banks will include this in the mortgage package.
- **Letting fees.**
- **Stamp duty:** This is the next biggest cost after your deposit; the amount you have to pay is a percentage of the purchase price.
- **Buildings insurance:** Shop around – you're not obliged to buy it from your mortgage provider. You may be covered if you pay a management or maintenance fee.

How much can you borrow?

When it comes to buy-to-let mortgages, each lender will vary in its product offerings. A loan-to-value (LTV) rate limit of 70% generally applies.

Some lenders will lend based on your personal income. However, with buy-to-let properties, lenders will primarily lend based on the rental income attainable from the property.

So, for example, a property that would generate a monthly rental income of €1,000 could support c. €125,000 of a loan amount where that represents a maximum of 70% of the purchase price in accordance with Central Bank rules. (See Chapter 3 for more information on these rules.)

Buy-to-let mortgages are usually open to Irish residents, both employed and self-employed, subject to the usual rules and limitations. In some cases, non-residents can apply.

The mortgage application process is similar to that of other applications. Both require documents such as proof of name and address, salary certificates and bank statements, etc.

One of the main differences between buy-to-let mortgages and standard residential mortgages is that the amount you can borrow is linked to the projected rental income.

With any property purchase, a standard valuation is a mandatory condition of the mortgage. However, I strongly advise you to get a detailed structural survey carried out prior to taking out the mortgage so as to identify any potential issues. Provided no deal-breakers are found in the survey, get an estimate of the repair costs involved and you can then use the information to negotiate a lower price for the mortgage.

Getting Ready to Rent

There are some things to consider before renting out your new property. Does the property need to be renovated to bring it to a minimum rentable standard? For example, does it need additional insulation, updating of the heating system, damp-proofing, etc.? What about furniture and appliances?

While you may choose to let the property out unfurnished, the rental price is usually slightly lower than that of furnished houses. Even then, unfurnished properties will still need basic fixtures, fittings and kitchen appliances. You can write off some of these expenses against tax.[2] (See 'Tax Considerations'.)

Your Obligations as a Landlord

Your legal obligations as a landlord are governed by the Residential Tenancies Act 2004.[3]

Two of these obligations are cost related:

- Local property tax: A tax you must pay based on the market value of the property.
- Landlord's insurance, which is typically a requirement of the mortgage provider.

Other obligations include:

- You will need to register your property with the Residential Tenancies Board.[4]

---

2   Office of the Revenue Commissioners, 'Irish Rental Income', http://www. justice.ie/en/JELR/Pages/Guide-to-Residential-Tenancies-Act-2004.

3   Threshold, 'Residential Tenancies Act: A Quick Guide', https://www. threshold.ie/download/pdf/residential_tenancies_act_2004_a_quick_ guide.pdf.

4   Residential Tenancies Board, 'Beginning a Tenancy', https://onestop shop.rtb.ie/beginning-a-tenancy/.

- Provide your tenant(s) with a rent book or receipts for rent paid.

- Register with the Revenue Commissioners as a landlord.

- Insurance: Landlord's buildings insurance is mandatory and typically a condition under the terms of the mortgage agreement.

- Building Energy Rating (BER): You are required to get the property evaluated for its building energy rating or BER.[5] This rating scores the energy efficiency of the property on a scale of A to G with A being the most energy efficient. The BER will appear in the rental listing.

- Repairs: You will be required to keep the property to a reasonable standard and have repairs carried out promptly.

- Maintenance of property and garden, if any.

Don't forget to factor ongoing costs into your decision – these can add up!

- Management agency fees: Letting and/or management of the property. This is typically a percentage of the monthly rent.

- If you decide to take on the maintenance yourself, make sure you factor in the time and costs involved. These will

---

5   Sustainable Energy Authority of Ireland (SEAI), 'Building Energy Rating Certificate (BER)', https://www.seai.ie/energy-ratings/building-energy-rating-ber/.

depend on the age, size and condition of the house, or on the presence of a large garden. Be prepared to be called out at the weekend to look at a leaking pipe or a broken washing machine.

– Redecorating: Updating the heating system or installing insulation. Does the house need painting or replacement kitchen cabinets? A facelift may improve the overall rent you can charge.

– Gas safety certificate: If your property has gas-fired central heating or appliances you must have them serviced annually. You're obliged to provide your tenants with an up-to-date gas safety certificate from a registered engineer.

Rainy Day Fund

Make sure to keep some funds, like the rental deposit, aside for contingencies such as a busted boiler or washing machine repairs. It's a good idea to have three to six months' worth of mortgage payments built up to allow for when tenants move out, as it can take time to find the right renters for your property.

Short-term Lettings

It's important to keep in mind that banks will lend based on the long-term rent attainable from a property rather than the short-term rent attainable, even if the latter yields a higher amount of rent.

Tax Considerations

I recommend that you set up a separate bank account to manage the finances of the newly rented property. It's also essential that you get up to speed on your tax requirements.

- You'll have to pay income tax on your rental income, at 20% or 40% depending on your personal circumstances. However, several allowable expenses may be claimed against rental income for tax purposes, including local authority rates, insurance premiums of fire and public liability, and letting fees.[6]

- You can also claim a capital allowance of 12.5% per year over eight years for the costs of fixtures and fittings. These include furniture and white goods such as a dishwasher or fridge.

- Mortgage interest relief: As of January 2019, you can deduct 100% of the interest paid on your mortgage on a rental property. This is up from 85% in 2018, 80% in 2017 and 75% in previous years.[7]

- Capital gains tax: This applies when you sell the property and if the profit you make exceeds certain thresholds. Current rate is 33%.

6   Office of the Revenue Commissioners, 'Irish Rental Income: What expenses are allowed?', https://www.revenue.ie/en/property/rental-income/irish-rental-income/what-expenses-are-allowed.aspx.

7   Citizens Information, 'Housing Tax Credits and Reliefs', https://www.citizensinformation.ie/en/money_and_tax/tax/income_tax_credits_and_reliefs/housing_tax_credits_and_reliefs.html#lcf158.

After taking all this on board, let's take an example of an investor who purchases an apartment for €200,000. They incur 1% stamp duty on the purchase price, which is €2,000, as well as legal fees of €3,000. This means that the total outlay is €205,000. Some years later, the investor sells the apartment for €300,000. Auctioneers' fees are €7,000 and solicitor's fees €3,000, meaning the net proceeds of the sale are €290,000. The gain for the investor is €85,000 (i.e. the difference between the net proceeds of sale and the total acquisition cost). Capital gains tax is payable at the rate of 33% on this gain, which is €28,050.

At first glance, the buy-to-let process may seem daunting. However, an authorised mortgage advisor can guide you through the project, assisting you with cash-flow projections and offering advice on mortgage protection products. Once you know what you are getting into, investing in the buy-to-let market can be a smooth operation, as well as financially rewarding.

CHAPTER 7

SELF-BUILD

Building your own home is an ambitious undertaking. In other words, be prepared to set aside your evenings and weekends for the foreseeable future to get through to the end of this process.

Building projects are susceptible during construction to delays from planning paperwork and other setbacks, such as adverse weather conditions. On the upside, within reason and budget, you get to design your own home, choose the layout and room size, and decide on design features, from open-plan connected living space to hip roof.

Before you get the wheels in motion, take a look at other houses you like and browse through home-design magazines and websites to see what designs you prefer and how you'd like your home to be. However, a word of caution: if you're a fan of TV shows such as *Room to Improve* or *Grand Designs* you will know that it's not a good idea to get too hung up on minor details. You will inevitably have to make compromises to suit the layout and structure of the house and, of course, to ensure costs don't spiral out of control. It is essential that you stick as closely as possible to your budget. Any proposed changes should be carefully factored into the overall cost.

The mortgage process is a little more complex for a self-build than with a standard transaction where you buy a ready-made second-hand or new home. And there are many aspects to take into account, such as how you came by the site.

The Site: A Gift or a Purchase?

If you're lucky enough to be given a site as a gift from a parent, then you're well on your way to opening the door to your new home.

Just to note: it may be advisable, from a tax perspective, that the site be registered in the sole name of the person whose parents have gifted the site, and that the mortgage be then in both names in the case of joint borrowers. This can make sense from a tax point of view as the son or daughter who has received the gift will have an exemption from capital acquisitions tax up to a threshold of €320,000. Most banks who offer self-build mortgages will facilitate this joint-mortgage request with the site registered in one name. Still, it is advisable to obtain professional tax advice before making a decision.

If you are purchasing the site, however, things can get more complicated. In this case, there are several things you must take into consideration and do before even applying to purchase a site.

- Look at planning permission attached to the site. Some counties have local planning restrictions attached to sites in rural areas so that applicants for permission must be 'native' to the area, i.e. have lived locally for a specified number of years and/or demonstrated a local housing need. My advice is to avoid these areas if at all possible, unless you meet the criteria.

- Sites with planning permission already granted will generally cost more than sites that do not have planning permission granted.

- Research the Local Area Plans as these will include information on zoning and development schemes. They should be available at your local council offices.

- Register your interest with estate agents in the area.

- If you find a site you like, it's important to engage an engineer/surveyor and/or solicitor to ensure that the site benefits from a legal right of way and that the boundaries (which are basically the perimeter of the site) are clearly defined. Early advice can help avoid potential legal issues and other problems at a later stage.

- It is a huge advantage if a site has a dwelling in situ, even if the dwelling is derelict, as one should be able to convert/extend or replace the existing structure once the design is in keeping with local buildings.

Hiring the Team for the Build

- Do you want an architect or project manager to oversee the build? If you're choosing an architect, ask for recommendations from family and friends and make sure the person is certified. You can check on the website of the regulatory body – the Royal Institute of the Architects in Ireland (https://www.riai.ie).

- Get three quotes from building contractors and educate yourself as to the difference between an estimate and a quote. (A quote is the exact cost broken down into labour, materials, etc.)

- Two VAT rates apply here: 13.5% for labour and 23% for materials (except for ready-to-pour concrete and blocks, charged at 13.5%).

- The rates of some self-employed tradespeople could be under the VAT threshold, and they might be able to offer their services to you VAT free.

- Make sure each tradesperson's work is covered by guarantee and insurance, including public liability insurance.

'Opt in' or 'Opt out' Legislation

In 2015 an amendment to the Building Control Amendment Regulations (BCAR) brought about an option for those who are building their own home to 'opt in' or 'out' of the certification process.[1]

The certification process (opt in) is a statutory one, supported by an assigned designer and an assigned certifier

---

1   Department of Housing, Planning and Local Government, 'Building Control', https://www.housing.gov.ie/housing/building-standards/building-regulations/building-control.

appointed by you in their professional capacity to inspect and fully certify the various stages of the building works as compliant to building standards and regulations.

The reason the optional aspect was introduced was that professional fees for statutory certification were considered prohibitively high in some cases. So when you opt out, you do not have to get the building design or works certified and as a result can make savings on the fees for those services.

So, what does this mean for self-builders?

If you opt out of getting a certification, you have decided not to have a professional sign off on and certify the design and construction of the building. Instead, as the owner, you take on the roles of designer and certifier, and so the responsibility to ensure the building meets quality control standards falls on you.

How do I opt in?

You hire an assigned designer and certifier who lodge documents onto the Building Control Management System (BCMS).[2] The BCMS is an online database and administration resource that stores all documentation (forms, design and compliance certificates) relating to your project as evidence that your building was constructed and completed in adherence to building regulations.

---

2   National Building Control Office, 'Welcome to the Building Control Management System (BCMS)', https://www.localgov.ie/en/bcms.

How do I opt out?

You must file your commencement notice yourself on BCMS and indicate that you are opting out of the certification process. This provides notice to Building Control Authorities of your intention to start works on your construction project. In this case, you will also need to supply the design drawings.

If you wish to appoint a main contractor, you can assign them to act as the builder, or you can appoint yourself and hire individual tradesmen to do the job.

In either case, I recommend that you follow the Sample Preliminary Inspection Plan for Single Dwellings, which is published by the Department of the Environment and sets out the stages serving as a homeowner's guide to building regulations when building a one-off house.[3]

So, ultimately, opting out means that you don't have to get the design or construction certified by a professional and can therefore avoid the fees associated with those services. On the other hand, as this is new legislation it's still unclear how it will affect the value of your house in the future. Furthermore, you will not be able to register a certificate of compliance on completion with your local authority, which may make things more complicated if you want to sell your house down

---

3   Department of Housing, Planning and Local Government, 'Sample Preliminary Inspection Plan', https://www.housing.gov.ie/sites/default/files/migrated-files/en/Publications/DevelopmentandHousing/BuildingStandards/FileDownLoad%2C41034%2Cen.pdf.

the line. As there will be no certificate of compliance, an opinion of compliance will have to be issued instead.

Therefore, while opting out can save you money in the short term, it is important to think carefully about your decision.

To summarise: if you are to opt out you will need to carry out the following:

- Submit a commencement notice to your local authority on the BCMS portal.
- Declare your intention to opt out.
- Nominate a competent builder.
- Submit design drawings.
- Submit a documents schedule and compliance statement.

Your Obligations

Whatever your decision, whether you opt in or out of the certification requirements of the building control regulations, when you're building a new house or extension larger than 40 square metres you still need to comply with a number of regulations, including building regulations, health and safety, and planning laws.

In addition, you are expected to hire competent professionals for your project and ensure that they are registered. Under the terms of your mortgage agreement, your lender will need each stage of the building process signed off on. Typically this occurs at four to five key milestones in the build, for example, the completion of the floor, wall plate and roof levels, with the final sign-off upon the property's completion.

The Self-build Mortgage

Most lenders offer mortgages to those looking to build their own home or extensively renovate an existing property.

For a self-build you need a 10% deposit, or 20% if you're a second-time buyer as the 80% LTV rate applies.

If you have received the site as a gift, then you already have some equity in the property. For example, if the site valuation is €100,000, then the bank considers the full €100,000 as equity, so a deposit shouldn't be a problem, but if you're purchasing a site then it could be.

Self-build applicants are also eligible for the help-to-buy scheme. (See Chapter 5 for a detailed overview.) In summary, this allows the borrower (PAYE or self-assessed taxpayer) to claim a rebate of income tax of up to 5% of the build cost, once they meet the qualifying criteria.

Self-build mortgage approvals are generally valid for longer than the standard six months as the process is more complicated. Once you receive your letter of loan offer – i.e. the legal loan contract between the borrower and the lender – you will usually have up to twelve months' approval. This document outlines the loan amount, the term of the loan and the relevant interest rate.

Lenders typically offer the lower amount of the total value of the site purchase cost plus the build cost or the final value of the house upon completion. The final valuation will be carried out once the property is completed and the final certificate of compliance is issued by the supervising architect, engineer or surveyor. In the case of first-time buyers, this is 90% of site cost/value plus construction costs or 90% of valuation on completion. For second or subsequent buyers it's 80%, unless they qualify for a LTV exemption.

Staged Payments

The main difference between a standard and a self-build mortgage, basically, is that with the former the drawdown of the payment happens when the purchase completes, whereas with the latter the payments are staged according to agreed completed points in the project. These are usually four or five stage payments – often correlating with the 'sign-off stages' referenced earlier, i.e. floor level, wall plate level, roof level – with the final payment being retained by the lender pending final valuation.

Your assigned certifier, who is a registered architect, engineer or surveyor, will review and certify at each stage, from preparation of the site and laying foundations, to frame construction and completion of the plasterwork.

At the last stage the bank will require a final valuation report from the same person who carried out the initial valuation and a certificate of compliance issued by your architect, engineer or surveyor.

The advantage of the staged payments is that you pay

interest only on what you've drawn down and not on the entire mortgage, so the inevitable delays won't cost you too much more.

Self-build Checklist

The standard documentation, including:

- Photo identification.
- Proof of address.
- Marriage certificate (if applicable).
- Certificate of income – to be completed and stamped by employer.
- P60 or tax balancing statement for previous year.
- Payslips – three if paid monthly, six if fortnightly, etc.
- Current account statements – previous six months.
- Savings account statements – previous six months.
- Credit card statements – previous six months.
- Loan and/or mortgage statements – previous twelve months.

Plus …

1. Details of build costs.
2. Fixed contract quotation or detailed breakdown of each element of the project.
3. Planning permission – full, in place at mortgage application stage.

4. Initial valuation report by assigned certifier.

5. Evidence of your contribution: a statement of your savings account or a signed gift letter (if either the site or funds have been gifted). Ask your mortgage advisor what type of documentation your lender requires.

6. A Land Registry map – Ordnance Survey Ireland or similar – of the site.

I've also included some useful resources at the end of the book to help you with your decision regarding whether or not a self-build mortgage is the right move for you.

CHAPTER 8

OVERSEAS BUYERS

Who is an Overseas Buyer?

If you are an Irish citizen living abroad and looking to purchase a property in Ireland, you are considered an overseas buyer.

Types of Overseas Buyers

One group is returning emigrants. Over a decade since the economic downturn, many who moved to Canada, Australia, UAE, USA, UK, Europe and elsewhere for jobs are now looking to come home. Moving back to a home of your own is an appealing idea. Otherwise, if you return, some lenders will require you to be working in Ireland for up to six or twelve months before you are eligible to apply for a mortgage as a resident, as you would no longer fall under the category of overseas buyer and the lender will want to see continuity of employment for a period of time. In the latter case, you would also need to find alternative living accommodation in the meantime – an increasingly difficult prospect because of the high demand for rental properties.

Another type of overseas buyer, of course, includes

applicants intending to remain abroad but wanting a holiday home in Ireland. Once an applicant is an Irish citizen and has sufficient income to maintain their living expenses in the country where they are living, as well as any credit commitments, then they can apply for a holiday home mortgage to purchase a property in Ireland. They will be restricted to a maximum LTV of 65% and a maximum term of twenty-five years.

The intended use of the property determines the lending options for the borrower. The LTV available for overseas buyers is generally capped at around 65% to 70% of the purchase price of the property.

Playing by Different Rules

Those living outside of Ireland and seeking to purchase property here are subject to different mortgage rules than residents. Some banks treat non-resident applicants like investors, meaning that they pay a higher interest rate, while some banks will offer owner-occupier interest rates to overseas buyers on the basis that the property they are purchasing will be used as a holiday home.

Deposit requirements also differ from those of resident buyers. For example, a first-time buyer living in Ireland needs to have 10% (up to a limit) of the property value and a second or subsequent buyer needs 20%. An expat applicant, on the other hand, will need to come up with 35% or more, depending on the lender.

Overseas buying is on the rise. One in five enquiries about buying property in Ireland comes from people living abroad, according to a recent study.[1] In terms of enquiries by country, they say interest from UK residents has fallen in the aftermath of Brexit from 36% to 28%. Meanwhile, enquiries from United States residents represent over 22%, with residents of the Gulf States and Dubai also featuring.

What are the Restrictions?

The country you are applying from has an impact on the process. The EU Credit Directive of 2016 led to restrictions in this area.[2] All Irish banks will lend to people living in Ireland, but they may not lend to someone outside of the EU, whether they are an Irish citizen or not. This is largely due to the lack of facilities to transfer the mortgage into the currency of the country the borrower resides in.

Currently there are very few banks offering mortgages to Irish citizens living outside the EU, which makes it more challenging for potential buyers to obtain finance while they are living abroad.

---

1   Real Estate Alliance, 'One-in-five property enquiries from overseas – survey', https://www.realestatealliance.ie/news/detail/885590836675738 8639.

2   European Commission, 'Mortgage credit: Find information about EU rules on mortgage credit', https://ec.europa.eu/info/business-economy-euro/banking-and-finance/consumer-finance-and-payments/consumer-financial-services/credit/mortgage-credit_en#eurulesformortgagecredit.

Know the Rates

One of the main factors affecting the rates of deposit required for an overseas buyer is the intended use of the property. For example, a holiday home mortgage for Irish people living abroad has a LTV rate of 65%, and the related home loan interest rates are 1.5% to 2% lower than buy-to-let interest rates.

Let's look at an example.

An Irish citizen living outside the EU wants to purchase a property in Ireland but is unsure whether he wants a buy-to-let or to use it as a holiday home. If he opts for the former, his interest payment rate could be up to 4.5%. Based on a €300,000 loan amount over twenty-five years, his monthly payment is €1,667 or €20,010 annually or €500,250 over the twenty-five-year period. If he chooses the latter, however, he can secure a home loan interest rate. Let's say, in this case, the maximum LTV available is 65% and the variable interest rate currently available at this LTV is 2.95% – this gives a monthly repayment of €1,415, which is €16,978 annually or €424,452 over the twenty-five-year period – a significant difference. Based on a €300,000 loan over a twenty-five-year period, the difference between the investment and home loan rates is €253 monthly, €3,036 annually, or €75,900 over the twenty-five-year term.

So, taking this into consideration, you can see why you should seriously think about the intended use of the property prior to applying for a mortgage!

Overseas Buyers' Checklist

If you're living overseas and considering buying a property in Ireland, you will need to get your paperwork in order. This includes:

- Photo I.D.
- Proof of address.
- Your P60 or tax balancing statement for the previous year.
- Payslips for the past three months.
- A certificate of income stamped by your employer.
- Statements for the last six months for the following: current account, savings account and credit card.
- Mortgage statement for the last twelve months.
- Copy of your credit history from Ireland.
- Copy of your credit history from the country where you are currently residing.
- Your CV.
- Copy of your marriage certificate, if applicable.

If you are self-employed, additional documents are required:

- Three years of certified accounts.

- A tax clearance certificate.
- Bank statements for business current, savings and credit card accounts for the last six months.
- Three Form 11 equivalents (tax returns summary) for the last three years.
- Three self-assessment equivalents for the last three years.

Overall, when it comes to overseas buyers, it's important to remember that your residing in a different country will impact on your application: this includes factors like deposit requirements and the currency of your income, as well as the intended use of the property.

Basically, applications from overseas buyers can be tricky so, before making a move, I recommend getting the advice of a trusted and experienced broker to begin discussing your options.

CHAPTER 9

SWITCHING

Just like you shop around for a cheaper or better car insurance company or electricity provider, it's worth reviewing mortgage providers every few years to see if you can make savings.

What is Switching?

Switching is the term used to describe the process of changing mortgage provider. This is usually done to get a lower interest rate on your mortgage from a new lender with a view to saving money on interest.

Some people go through the entire term of their mortgage without considering whether their lender is offering them the best rate. However, it is prudent to review the terms of your mortgage on a regular basis – perhaps as part of a wider financial 'health-check'. You don't need to switch every year, but it's a financially savvy move to take the time to consider the current market, the value of your property and the interest rates on offer from all lenders on an ongoing basis.

My Neighbour is doing it – can I?

The answer is, most likely, yes. I estimate that one in every three mortgage holders would save by switching. (I am not including European Central Bank-related tracker interest rates in these figures as they currently offer low interest rates given that the ECB base rate is 0%, meaning a typical tracker mortgage interest rate is approximately 1% and such mortgages have not been available in Ireland since 2008.)

If you have been on the same rate for more than three years, or you are coming to the end of a fixed rate period, then you should certainly review your options.

Regardless of whether you are a variable *or* a fixed rate mortgage holder, you could potentially save tens of thousands of euro over the remaining term.

The Myths and Misconceptions

- 'I can't switch if I'm on a fixed rate.' Not true. You can break a fixed rate contract. You may be charged a breakage fee by your lender, but the savings you make upon switching, plus, potentially, any cashback offer from a new lender, could more than cover the charges. In addition, due to the current low cost of funds available for banks, many don't impose a fee for exiting a fixed rate contract. You will need to call your bank to check this, however.

Mick and Fiona, for example, have a home loan with €300,000 outstanding. They are currently on a fixed rate of 3.6% for the next two years with twenty-eight years left on their mortgage term. They contact their bank to check the early fixed rate breakage fee and are advised that the fee is €1,050. They contact a mortgage broker who advises them that if they switch lender, he can obtain a two-year fixed rate of 2.3%, which will reduce their monthly payment from €1,418 to €1,211, with a saving of €207 monthly or €2,484 annually or €4,968 over the two-year period. So, in this example, even though Mick and Fiona are liable to pay a breakage fee of €1,050, it is worthwhile as they will save €4,968 over the next two years alone.

Before Switch	After Switch
Fixed 2-yr interest rate 3.6%	Fixed 2-yr interest rate 2.3%
Monthly repayment €1,418	Monthly repayment €1,211
	Total savings over term €4,968*

* savings excluding breakage fee

- **'I need to have a LTV of less than 80% on my home.'** Again, not true. While some lenders will offer you a better rate according to the amount of equity you have built up, you can still switch if your LTV is between 80% and 90%.

- **'Switching is a long and difficult process.'** Not true. Switching can be straightforward with the help of an expert, and some banks require less documentation for switchers than for a new application.

- **'I'll just end up spending any savings made on the legal costs of conveyancing.'** (Conveyance is the legal term for processing the paperwork involved in buying and selling a property and transferring the deeds of ownership.) Not true. You will know in advance, once you or your broker run the numbers, whether the savings made will outweigh any ancillary costs that may be incurred. If you stay with the same lender but move to a different rate, then you may not incur any additional costs.

Cashback on Switching

The impact can be significant. Let's look at Rua and Kerry's experience.

They took a €400,000 mortgage over thirty-five years at a three-year fixed interest rate of 3.6%. The interest rate they selected at the time of drawdown was reasonably competitive and they also received upfront cashback from their lender. However, their rate is now changing to a higher variable rate of 4.2%. Their payments will be going from €1,676 to €1,802 monthly. They tried to negotiate a lower variable rate with their current lender without success, so they have decided to switch to a lower variable rate of 2.95% with another lender, which will reduce their monthly payments to €1,534. This will save them €268 monthly or €3,216 annually or €102,912 over the remaining thirty-two years of their mortgage. In addition, they will receive €2,000 from the new lender, which covers the legal fees involved in switching.

Before Switch	After Switch
Fixed 3-yr interest rate 3.6%	Variable interest rate 2.95%
Monthly repayment €1,802	Monthly repayment €1,534
	Total savings over term €102,912

What will I need?

If you decide to proceed with switching, you will need to go through the mortgage application process and submit your documentation. This varies from lender to lender. Typically, you will require the following documents:

- Passport identification.
- One recent payslip, P60 or tax balancing statement and salary certificate.
- Three/six months recent current account statements – depends on lender requirement.
- Most recent credit card statements if applicable – last one, three or six, depending on lender.
- Most recent mortgage statement.
- Relevant application form and bank declaration.

Where do I start?

- Contact your existing lender to confirm your rate of interest, balance outstanding and term remaining on the mortgage.

- If you are on a fixed rate, ask your lender what fee, if any, they charge for breaking the mortgage contract.

- Ask your current lender to review your interest rate and enquire about variable and fixed rate options for an existing customer.

- Contact a mortgage broker and ask them to compare your existing mortgage terms to what's on the market. (Technically, you can do this research yourself, but it will mean numerous calls to multiple lenders, so in reality it's probably not the easiest route for you to take.) The more equity you have in your home, the better the new terms you'll be offered, but you can switch even if your loan is 90% of your value.

- Your broker can check what incentives other lenders are offering to switchers. The 'incentive' usually covers the legal costs, as well as any possible breakage fee, although this would need to be worked out on a case-by-case basis.

- Assess the best value option for you. A broker can run calculations on the interest rates you have been offered to see the potential savings you can make. This should not be a complex process. But there is market research to be done and there are lots of forms to be filled and boxes to be ticked. A broker will do all the legwork and calculations, communicate with lenders on your behalf and explain all of your options.

- You will need to decide whether to stick with your current lender or move to a different one. Moving to a different provider will mean going through the mortgage approval process again. Changing lenders can be relatively simple if you have expert help.

- Ultimately you need to ask yourself a question: Why would I stick with a lender that is not giving me the best value?

Take your time, weigh up all your options and seek expert advice in order to decide if switching is the best course of action.

How much can I save?

Again, as stated earlier in the chapter, switching to a lower interest rate can save you a considerable amount of money in the long term depending on the rate and capital amount.

Let me give you an example of savings on an interest rate reduction of 1.6%. By switching from a 4.2% rate to 2.6%, a mortgage holder with a loan of €350,000 over thirty years can save over €300 per month, €3,732 per year or €14,897 over four years.

Before Switch	After Switch
Variable interest rate 4.2%	Variable interest rate 2.6%
Monthly repayment €1,712	Monthly repayment €1,401
	Total savings over four years €14,897

In summary, it costs mortgage holders absolutely nothing to explore what 'switching' their mortgage can yield in terms of interest savings. I have sought to challenge and address any lack of knowledge or awareness by outlining the process and the financial benefit to be gained from taking this step.

People can often be put off by their first mortgage experience, which for many is stressful. However, the second time round should be a lot more straightforward. Yes, of course there will be forms to fill in, but the rewards for this bit of administration can be in the region of thousands and life-changing as a result.

CHAPTER 10

TRADING UP

Your family has outgrown the starter home you bought ten or fifteen years ago. You may require more storage space, an extra bedroom or a larger garden. Could now be the right time to make a move to a property more suited to your needs?

Before you take that step onto the next rung of the property ladder, it's crucial that you do your research to determine the best mortgage solution for your needs now and into the future, keeping in mind your current outgoings and financial commitments.

Hold on to your Cash

If you are thinking about trading up, it's wise to keep your powder dry, i.e. hold on to your cash reserves. Lenders want to see that you have several months of reserves to cover your mortgage repayments in the event of unexpected expenses and in order to avoid early default; most require at least two months' worth of repayments being held in reserve but prefer more. Just to be clear, cash or liquid assets include balances in current and savings accounts and investments such as stocks, shares or bonds.

There are a few actions you can take to free up cash, if required, so you have the requisite cash reserves:

- Stop overpaying your mortgage now. If you've been paying extra every month or on an ad-hoc basis to reduce the term of your mortgage, bring your repayments back to the terms of the mortgage agreement. Use that extra cash to build up your savings.

- Don't use cash reserves to make any sizeable purchases. If you absolutely need to change your car, for example, take out the maximum loan over the longest period and at the lowest interest rate instead.

- Delay making any unnecessary purchases using cash or credit until after the mortgage process has been finalised.

You've done the groundwork – reduced your outgoings, built up your savings – but you're still struggling to come up with the 20% deposit required as you are a non-first-time buyer.

An example can help show the way.

Jacob and April plan to sell their two-bedroom apartment for €300,000 and buy a four-bedroom house for €400,000. Because they are second-time buyers, they are limited to a loan amount of €320,000 (i.e. 80% LTV). They have €50,000 cash savings. However, they need to sell their existing apartment to fund the balance of the deposit. Their loan on the apartment is *c*. €200,000 so they should net *c*. €90,000 after selling expenses such as auctioneers and legal fees have been deducted.

This process of selling one property and purchasing another simultaneously can be challenging, so some people will firstly sell their existing property in order to have cash in the bank. Then, they either move in with family or rent a property so that they are a stronger buyer for the house that they wish to trade up to and are not dependent on the sale of their existing property.

Central Bank Rules for Second-Time Buyers

I've covered these rules in Chapter 3, but here's a brief summary:

In February 2015, after the financial crisis, the Central Bank introduced a range of measures for mortgages aimed at maintaining financial stability and protecting consumers.[1] The measures set limits on the size of mortgages that consumers can borrow based on loan-to-value (LTV) and loan-to-income (LTI). Under LTI rules, a limit of 3.5 times gross income applies to all borrowers. First-time buyers can borrow up to 90% of the property value. Second-time and

---

1 'Explainer – What are the Mortgage Measures?', https://www.central bank.ie/consumer-hub/explainers/what-are-the-mortgage-measures.

subsequent buyers can borrow 80% of the property value only, which of course also applies to people looking to trade up.

What about Negative Equity?

The 80% rule is based on the assumption that owner-occupiers looking to trade up will have equity from their current dwelling to put towards the next one. However, the collapse in the property market left many first-time buyers stuck in negative equity limbo for a decade or more. Negative equity occurs when your property is valued at less than the amount that you owe on your mortgage. (See Chapter 13 for more information.)

However, the good news is that as a result of a surge in house prices in recent years, the percentage of Irish borrowers trapped in negative equity has fallen from 40% to 10%.[2] Contrary to popular belief, a person whose property is in negative equity is entitled to apply for a mortgage on another property and may well be approved for the loan amount sought once they meet the relevant lender's credit policy.

Exemptions

If you've explored all avenues and still can't come up with the

---

2 'Residential Property Price Index December 2018', https://www. cso.ie/en/releasesandpublications/ep/p-rppi/residentialpropertyprice indexdecember2018/additionalindicators.

20% deposit, you may be able to avail of an exemption. There are two types of exemptions available, *but* lenders may grant an exemption under the LTV rule *or* the LTI rule, *not both*.

I've found that most of the applications for exemptions to the Central Bank rules are from second-time buyers.

Loan-to-Value

Lenders can apply exemptions up to 20% of the total value of home loans that they grant to second-time and subsequent buyers. This means that it's possible for second-time buyers to borrow up to 90% of the purchase price, reducing the deposit required to 10%.

Under current rules, someone trading up to a house with a purchase price of €350,000 would require a deposit of €70,000, but just €35,000 if they got the exemption that meant the LTV increased to 90%. Similarly, a house valued at €550,000 would need a deposit of €110,000 under the rules, but just €55,000 if the LTV rose to 90%.[3]

Loan-to-Income

Under LTI exemptions, lenders can circumvent the 3.5 times gross income rule in 10% of second-time cases. It is possible to get the gross income multiple increased to four or even

---

3   'Mortgages: How to Get Around the Central Bank's Borrowing Rules', *The Irish Times*, 19 April 2016, https://www.irishtimes.com/business/financial-services/mortgages-how-to-get-around-the-central-bank-s-borrowing-rules-1.2614954.

4.5 times an applicant's combined annual gross income (i.e. before tax).

Being granted an exemption of this kind can make a significant difference to the amount you can borrow. For example, a couple with a combined income of €100,000 can borrow €350,000 under the rules. If they can get an LTI exemption, they can potentially borrow up to €450,000.

Take the example of Mary, who previously owned an apartment with an ex-boyfriend. She wants to buy a house now. Despite saving hard for two years and keeping a clean credit and banking record, she's 2% to 3% short of the 20% deposit.

An opportunity has come up to buy her dream house and at a great price, as the sellers are emigrating and are looking to sell quickly. Lenders tend to prefer applicants who have a particular property in mind and will complete the transaction in the short term. With the assistance of a good broker, buyers like Mary who tick the right boxes may be able to secure an exemption from their bank under either the LTV or LTI rule.

Decisions are made on a case-by-case basis. Most lenders will require a minimum level of income; for example, a sole applicant will need an income of €40,000 or joint applicants should be earning at least €70,000, but this varies from bank to bank.

Remember, as stated earlier, you can apply for either a greater LTI multiple or a higher LTV, but not both.

Note: If you receive an exemption on the LTI rule, which allows you to increase the amount you can borrow, you will need a bigger deposit.

It's also worth noting that if the gap between what you need to borrow and what you can borrow under the current rules is relatively small, e.g. €10,000 or so, it's unlikely your bank will 'give up' an exemption as it's the whole loan that is classified as an exemption as opposed to just the amount of €10,000 over 3.5 times the income.

In conclusion, trading up can be more straightforward than people may think. There are ways to navigate obstacles such as negative equity and deposit requirements, and with the right advice from an authorised mortgage broker, who will navigate you through this process, approval can be obtained even if your situation is not clear-cut at the outset.

CHAPTER 11

TRADING DOWN

Trading down is more challenging than you might think. Typically, homeowners looking to downsize are mature people and are called 'empty nesters' with large family homes that are no longer suitable for their needs. The four-bedroomed Celtic Tiger home and sprawling garden in which you've raised your family feels too big now the kids have flown the nest. With retirement on the horizon you're ready to begin the next chapter in your life.

Whether you're hoping to fulfil a long-held dream of retiring to a cottage in the country, an apartment in the city or a bungalow with a sea view, you should consider the personal and financial implications. It's a life-changing decision, so take time to think it through, and weigh up the advantages and disadvantages of downsizing.

The Pros

Reduced running costs: With a smaller property you will see significant savings on energy bills, insurance, maintenance costs and property tax.

Lump sum: Downsizers often have their mortgage paid off, and as proceeds from the sale of your principal residence are free from capital gains tax, this could be a sizable chunk, if you're prudent. You can use this windfall to invest in stocks or other financial products, give your pension a boost, or help your adult children with a deposit for their own place.

Lower mortgage: If you're still paying off your mortgage, moving to a smaller home will mean lower monthly repayments and/or reduced term.

More time: A large house with a garden needs a lot of upkeep. Moving to a smaller home frees up time to devote to hobbies, family, travel and social life, etc.

Be closer to grandchildren: You may want to move nearer to your adult children to help out with grandchildren.

Being a cash buyer: While there is a shortage of smaller dwellings such as bungalows and two-bed houses on the market, as a cash buyer who has just sold a property, you have a significant advantage over mortgage applicants. Almost half of all properties bought in Ireland in 2018 were with cash or savings.[1] Furthermore, an estimated 23% of cash

---

1   MyHome.ie Property Report, Q4 2018: https://media.myhome.ie/content/propertyreport/2018/Q42018/MyHomePropertyReportQ4-2018.pdf.

buyers in 2016 were downsizers according to Savills' 2017 report data.[2]

The Cons

Emotional ties: You may have lived in your current home for decades, watched your children grow up and move out, and formed bonds with neighbours and ties with the community. It can be difficult to leave the familiar behind.

Hidden costs: Beware of additional costs, which can chip away at your nest egg. These extras can add up and reduce the overall sum. So, before you decide to sell, calculate carefully, including costs such as estate agent fees and stamp duty in the final tally.

Having weighed up the options, you've made your decision: you're ready to downsize. So, what now? Here are some factors to consider:

- Staying within your neighbourhood/community makes for a smoother transition. You have ties to the area and are familiar with local GP, shops and other services.

---

2 'Housing: Who are the cash buyers and how come there's so many of them?', *The Irish Times*, 19 September 2017, https://www.irishtimes.com/business/personal-finance/housing-who-are-the-cash-buyers-and-how-come-there-s-so-many-of-them-1.3224402.

- Urban or rural? Do you dream of a quiet country cottage, a city centre apartment, or a bungalow with a sea view?
- If you're considering a move to a new locality, research the current market value for similar properties in the area, look at development plans, amenities and services.
- If possible, look for a short-term rental as a trial. If this isn't an option, visit the area of your prospective new home at various times of the day or invest in a few overnight stays to get a feel for the area.
- If you're considering a property in a new housing development, ask the estate agent for the buyer profile. You may not want to be the only retired couple living in a complex among young families.
- Check out if there are many local clubs and activities. Joining community-based groups will help you to integrate into your new community.

Can I afford it?

Before that 'For sale' sign goes up, crunch the numbers. An independent mortgage specialist will guide you through the process, from planning the sale of your home to the purchase of a new one.

- Get your property valued by an independent professional.
- Avoid surprises: Factor in the estimated sale value of your house and other expenses including solicitor's fees, stamp duty, movers, storage, etc.

- Negotiate: Don't settle for the first offer for your old home; likewise, be prepared to haggle on the asking price for your desired property.

- Legalities: It's worth hiring an experienced conveyancing solicitor to coordinate the selling of a home and buying of another.

- Be prepared for delays: Land Registry paperwork can take a number of months to complete.

Finding the Right Property

Once you've decided on the area you want to move to, the next step is choosing a property. There are a number of elements to consider:

Affordability: Factor in additional costs such as annual maintenance fees for common areas, security system monitoring and service charges.

Future proofing: Calculate the cost of essential upgrades before committing to buying. Changes such as installing insulation, replacing windows or a new heating system can significantly add to the purchase price.

Additional costs: Don't forget other outlays such as the costs of redecorating and updating appliances – these can add up.

Energy ratings: Check out the energy ratings of your potential property – these are provided in the property listings. This can give you an idea of heating costs and of whether insulation or windows need to be upgraded.

Health and mobility issues: Is the property close to services such as a doctor's office, supermarket, banks and transport links? Does the structure allow for adaptations for needs in the future?

Be open to compromise: If you have specific requirements, such as the orientation of a property, it will make finding your new home harder.

Should I sell first?

Downsizers typically have their mortgage paid off or they're nearing the end of their mortgage. One example would be a couple nearing retirement living in a house worth €600,000. Their mortgage is paid off and they're looking to trade down to a house worth €300,000. They intend to use the surplus €300,000 to buy a holiday home, invest in a rental property or add to their retirement fund.

However, they may need to sell their existing home first to use the funds to purchase the second house. Logistically, this is a challenge.

Nevertheless, they could secure a mortgage for a lower amount on the new house, say 50% to 70% of LTV, if they could raise a deposit of 30% to 50% of the €300,000. Then they could buy the second house before selling the first.

At the same time, as they're close to retirement, their age could go against them, as the maximum age at the end of the repayment term is seventy. As a result, it may be easier to sell the house first, and then go about buying the second house.

Alternatives to consider

If you're unsure about moving or if the timing isn't right for you, there are alternatives to consider.

- **Staying put:** Consult with family members before making the move. You can change your mind. Personal circumstances may play a role in your decision, for example, if adult children may want to move back temporarily while they save for a deposit for a home of their own.

- **Rent out a room:** If you decide to take in students you can avail of generous tax breaks. Under the Revenue's rent-a-room relief scheme, you can earn up to €14,000 per year tax-free. Additionally, if you're over sixty-five, you don't begin to pay tax until earnings exceed €18,000 or €36,000 for a couple.

- **Convert:** You could also investigate whether converting part of your house into a self-contained unit for rental might be feasible.

- **Review grant options for upgrades and adaptations** (see Chapter 5).

It's important to review the pros and cons of trading down before making a decision, as while the prospect of trading down may be appealing from a financial point of view, it may not make as much sense from a lifestyle point of view if you are moving location, perhaps further away from your family, friends and community. Your choice will become clearer once you've weighed up all of the things that matter to you.

III

FURTHER MORTGAGE CONSIDERATIONS

CHAPTER 12

THE LEGAL PROCESS

Conveyancing is the legal term for the transfer of the title of a property from one party to another. There is a specific legal process involved in purchasing a property. Each stage should be completed before proceeding to the next. Prior to taking these steps, however, there are some things you should know.

What is the Title?

Title establishes the ownership of the property. In Ireland, there are two types of title: Land Registry title (registered) and Registry of Deeds title (unregistered).[1]

A property registered in the Land Registry will have a numbered folio that is evidence of ownership. The documentation contains the name and address of the owner, a description of the property and a map of the property or file plan.

A Registry of Deeds title is where deeds have been used to transfer the ownership of unregistered land or property.

---

1   Property Registration Authority, 'Land Registry Services', https://www. prai.ie.

Documentation includes deeds of conveyance used to transfer freehold or deeds of assignment in leasehold transfers.

Is the Property Freehold or Leasehold?

In Ireland, land is generally one or the other. Freehold is absolute ownership, whereas leasehold is where the purchaser is granted a lease for a specified number of years by the freehold owner. You need to know which type your potential property is before approaching a solicitor.

Pre-contractual Enquiries

There are some other enquiries and tasks that you must also undertake before beginning the legal process. This includes a planning search. Your local authority office is your first port of call for this, as you need to consult the Local Area Plan to find out how the property is zoned; if it's residential, commercial or otherwise; if there are any proposals for road schemes in the area, and if there were any previous planning permission applications granted or rejected. You should also check if there are any compulsory purchase orders in place that affect the property.

Other relevant searches include protected structure, public rights of way and tree preservation.

Once these enquiries and requisitions have been completed it's on to the next step.

Step-by-Step Guide

I've put together a step-by-step guide to help you to understand how it works once you have found a house you want:

1. Find a solicitor with conveyancing experience. Ask for recommendations from friends and family members, if necessary.

2. Is the property new or second-hand? A house or an apartment? New builds require two contracts: a building agreement and a contract for the transfer of the site. Your solicitor should advise you on this – which brings me to the next step.

3. Who is selling? Is the property being offered through private treaty, a developer – in the case of new builds – or by public auction? Arrange a viewing with the seller or estate agent in the case of private treaty or developer. If it is for sale by public auction, have your solicitor accompany you.

4. Instruct your solicitor to carry out preliminary investigations, including contracts for sale as well as title before the auction or before you make an offer. By this stage you will – hopefully – have already approached your bank and submitted a mortgage application. You will need to have approval in place before the date of the auction or before you put in an offer.

5. Hire an engineer to carry out a full structural survey. (See Chapter 15 for more detail on this.) I advise you to get this done as early as possible and certainly

before the auction or before you go 'sale agreed'. If you're serious about a property you will need to know if it has any significant structural issues before committing to purchase.

6. The day of the auction. If you are successful and your bid is accepted, then you are 'sale agreed'. With a private sale, this is where the vendor has accepted your offer.

7. When the hammer falls and the auctioneer says 'SOLD', the successful bidder (you) is committed to the purchase. You will need to pay a deposit straight-away and the balance within a specified time – usually one month. With private sales, you would be making an offer at this stage.

8. At this stage, you are required to pay a refundable booking deposit to the auctioneer or estate agent. You do not have any legally binding contract at this point.

9. The auctioneer or estate agent issues sales letters to you and the vendor, and your respective solicitors. The notes will include the prices and your details and those of the vendor.

10. The vendor's solicitor prepares contracts for sale and issues them to your solicitor with supporting title documentation.

11. Your solicitor examines the contracts and title and raises some pre-contract enquiries and requisitions to title.

12. The vendor's solicitor responds to any queries raised.

13. Having received the vendor's responses, and if both parties are in agreement, you are ready to sign the contract with your solicitor and send it to the vendor.

14. The vendor then signs the contract. Now that both parties have signed the contracts, the transaction is legally binding.

15. Once funds are available a closing date is arranged. Your solicitor will then carry out final searches on the property. These include a Land Registry or Registry of Deeds search to establish the ownership of the property, the title, existing mortgages, rights of residence or other restrictions. Other searches include a company search (carried out in the Companies Registration Office) if you are buying a new build – second-hand properties are generally private sales. Checks should be carried out to rule out any judgements made against the property or owner including claims under bankruptcy, sheriff and revenue cases.

16. If you and your solicitor are satisfied that everything is in order, you can instruct your lender to draw down your mortgage capital.

17. Once the sale is complete, your solicitor registers you as the new owner with the Land Registry. The deed of transfer is issued and you pay the stamp duty through your solicitor.

18. You receive the keys to your new home.

19. Moving-in day!

Outside of these steps, of course, there are other aspects of the legal process that you should be aware of. These include:

The Legislation

There are several pieces of legislation governing the sale of residential property in Ireland. These two Acts are the most important:

Statute of Frauds (Ireland) Act, 1695

Section 2 of this statute sets out that the agreement for the sale and the purchase of property must be in writing and include details of the parties, property and price paid.[2] Generally, conveyances go by the Law Society's standard form and conditions of sale.

Family Home Protection Act, 1976[3]

This Act limits the right of the owner to sell the family home without the prior consent of his or her non-owning spouse.

The Contract

A contract for the sale of the property will provide for the following:

---

2 Irish Statute Book, 'Statute of Frauds 1695', http://www.irishstatutebook. ie/eli/1695/act/12/section/2/enacted/en/html.

3 Irish Statute Book, 'Family Home Protection Act, 1976', http://www. irishstatutebook.ie/eli/1976/act/27/enacted/en/html.

- The consent of the vendor's non-owning spouse for the sale of the family home.
- Includes the names and addresses of the parties.
- Sets out the purchase price and deposit required.
- States the closing date agreed by the parties to the contract. On this date, the purchase money is paid and the deeds and keys to the property handed over.
- Lists the documents exchanged during the pre-contractual stages.
- Contains some standard conditions including the procedure for a property bought and sold at auction and warranties – in particular, full and appropriate planning permission on any property built since 1 October 1964. (See 'Further Points to Note'.)

Additional Costs

When you are buying a house, apart from the purchase price, there are several ancillary costs involved.

- Solicitor's fees are among these and can vary; therefore it is important to choose a solicitor who specialises in conveyancing. When asking for a quote, ask for a breakdown of the charges, which should include registry fees and VAT. Fees are usually around 1% of the purchase price.
- Search fees: These charges vary according to the number and extent of enquiries required.
- Registration fee: Costs to register the title with the Registry of Deeds or Land Registry.

(See Chapter 5 for more information on additional costs.)

Further Points to note

Rights over the Land

When purchasing a second-hand property, you should be aware that other people may have pre-existing rights of use over the land. These are known as 'easements'. Examples include rights of way or to fish in a pond on the property, or access to a beach or other public amenity.

Another type of easement is called 'profits-à-prendre', which means the right to take from another's land. Examples include the right to cut turf or timber, fish, carry out evacuations or extract minerals.

Easements should be established during the requisitions on title searches carried out during the contract stages.

Fixtures and Fittings

Fixtures and fittings are considered to be included as part of the sale unless an exclusion is included in the contract.

Planning Permission

Properties built after 1 October 1964 require planning permission. Your solicitor will check to make sure the documentation is in order. You will need to get an architect to certify that the house was built in accordance with the planning permission's conditions.

House or Apartment?

There are three main differences between buying a house and an apartment in Ireland.

- The title of an apartment is leasehold, rather than freehold.
- As the apartment is part of a building, it includes common areas.
- A management company will be responsible for maintenance of these common areas, e.g. hall, stairs, landscaping, etc. for which an annual fee is charged. Certain conditions and restrictions will apply to residents.

Hopefully all the information given in this chapter has provided you with a better, more rounded understanding of the legal process when buying a property.

CHAPTER 13

NEGATIVE EQUITY

What is Negative Equity?

The term 'negative equity' describes the situation when the market value of your property is less than the balance you owe on your mortgage. This means that if you want to sell your house, the proceeds from the sale will not cover your outstanding debt.

If your home has dropped in value since you bought it, you could be in negative equity. Newer buyers who bought during the boom (mid-1990s–late 2000s) are most affected, as they haven't paid off much of the capital on their mortgage.

While negative equity is not an ideal situation to be in, there are actions you can take to get out of it.

Many people who purchased properties during the 'Celtic Tiger', when house prices reached record highs, found themselves in negative equity when the recession hit and property prices fell significantly over a relatively short period of time. Properties have since, for the most part, regained their value, and the numbers of those in negative equity has fallen significantly in recent years.

Am I in Negative Equity?

For many homeowners it may not matter. In fact, you might not even know you are in negative equity. If you are reviewing your mortgage or considering moving and suspect your home has dropped in value, have a look at your last mortgage statement to calculate how much remains outstanding on your mortgage. Or contact your lender and request a current statement.

Next, get your home valued. Depending on the nature of the request, an estate agent may provide this without charge, for example, if you're exploring the prospect of selling. Let's look at an example:

Rebecca and Cali bought a house for €300,000 and borrowed 90% of this, which is €270,000. However, they have just found out that there's a new planning application nearby that will introduce significant levels of heavy traffic congestion, which will adversely affect the value of their property. They believe the value of their property is now €260,000 so they are in negative equity to the tune of €10,000. Should they decide to sell their property now, they will need to come up with cash of €10,000 to clear the negative equity portion of their mortgage. Alternatively, they can wait to see if the value is going to recover while the mortgage reduces as they continue to make their monthly repayment, and sell at a later date when the loan amount falls below the market value.

Taking on Negative Equity

It can pay to be patient. The pragmatic thing is to stay in your current property, if it meets your needs and you are managing the repayments. In a few years, when you have paid off more of your mortgage capital and the market value of your property increases, you will likely be back in the black.

Overpaying your Mortgage

If you're impatient to restore the balance, there is a way to do this quickly: you can overpay on your mortgage as long as it doesn't put you under financial pressure.

By making extra payments, you will start to reduce your negative equity quickly. But before you start to do this, check whether your mortgage provider will let you make overpayments and, if so, how much you can overpay without incurring a penalty.

You can also reduce your negative equity by making a lump sum payment, using savings if you can afford it, or money from an inheritance or a work-related bonus.

Both solutions depend on the arrangement you have with your lender. Check the terms and conditions. If in doubt, arrange a meeting with your mortgage advisor to see about renegotiating the terms.

There is no upper limit on the amount you can overpay on a variable rate or a fixed rate. However, a breakage fee may apply if overpaying on a fixed rate. The calculation for the breakage fee will be outlined in your loan agreement with the bank. Some banks will allow you to overpay a portion of your mortgage annually with an early breakage fee, even if your mortgage is subject to a fixed rate. Some banks will cap the breakage fee at the equivalent of six months' interest.

To demonstrate the impact of the 'overpay strategy' on term reduction and interest savings, let's look at Jenny and Ollie.

Jenny and Ollie have a €300,000 mortgage over thirty-five years at a variable interest rate of 3.15%. The monthly repayment on this is €1,179.81 with total interest of €195,520. If the couple were to overpay €100 monthly, this would reduce the term of their mortgage by four years and seven months and the total interest paid to €166,393. Taking it a step further, if they paid €300, then the term of their mortgage would be reduced by ten years and ten months and the total interest payable would be €128,797 – saving them €66,724 in interest.

Mortgage	Term	Current Interest Rate	Monthly Payment €	Overall Interest €	Monthly Overpay	Term Reduction	Overall Interest €	Total Savings €
€300,000	35	3.15%	1,180	195,520	100	55 mths	166,393	29,127
				195,520	300	130 mths	128,797	66,724

Renting out your Home

If you need to move for work or personal reasons, then you could become a landlord while you wait for a more favourable time to sell.

Renting out your property to cover your mortgage payments would allow you to rent a more suitable property elsewhere. While you may not have planned to be a renter again, it is a short-term solution until your negative equity is reduced to a more manageable level.

Your mortgage was likely approved as a principal dwelling, so if you are planning on renting it out then you will need to inform your mortgage provider of the change of use. Be aware that your lender may switch you to a higher interest rate in this instance. If you do decide to rent out your home, you will also need to inform your insurer and register as a landlord – which has tax implications.

When Negative Equity becomes a Problem

Negative equity becomes an immediate problem if you want or need to sell your home. Unless you have savings to repay the difference between the value of your home and the mortgage, you might find yourself stuck and unable to move. Negative equity can hinder your chances if you want to remortgage or switch to a fixed rate or a cheaper deal.

If you need to sell your property, the first step to take is to review your circumstances. If you are not up to date with your mortgage repayments, then you should be speaking to your lender's arrears team. Otherwise, you may be able to discuss your options around selling your home. Your lender will look at your level of negative equity, the approximate value of the type of property you want to move to and whether you can raise a deposit.

Some lenders operating in the Irish market do offer 'negative equity mortgages', but they typically limit the offer to their own customers. Speak to your current lender. They may let you transfer your negative equity to a mortgage on a new property, but you will still be expected to come up with a deposit.

Negative Equity Mortgages

Negative equity mortgages mean you can move without having to pay off the negative equity portion on your mortgage in advance – this is particularly useful if you can't put off a move.

Negative equity mortgages are tailored and generally pitched at people who own apartments that are in negative equity but who want to move to a larger property or house. The option could suit parents who need more space for their growing family, or if you have to relocate due to job commitments. It could also be an option if you're in negative equity in your current home and want to build your own home.

Since the introduction of the Central Bank mortgage lending rules in 2015, borrowers in negative equity have been exempt from the requirement to meet the loan-to-value (LTV) element. So, if you are buying a new home and selling your existing property, you could borrow on an LTV above 100% given that you are also carrying debt with you from your current home. Transferring the balance over means that you may remain in negative equity in your new property. Negative equity mortgages are still limited by the loan-to-income (LTI) rule, however, which is 3.5 times your salary.

Be aware that if you take out a negative equity mortgage, you may incur an early repayment charge or extra fees. In addition, your new mortgage may have a higher interest rate than your existing one.

Providers that supply negative equity mortgages offer two types:

Trading Up – The value of the new property is higher than that of your existing home. The LTV of the new mortgage (including the residual debt being carried from the property being sold) must be lower than that of the existing property.

Trading Down – The value of the new property you are hoping to purchase is lower than or equal to that of your existing home. The total new mortgage (including the negative equity being carried from the property being sold) must be equal to or less than the mortgage on the existing property.

Negative equity mortgages are generally only available to owner-occupiers and are not offered to those with buy-to-let mortgages. While these mortgages give you the chance to move on from your negative equity, you should look at the total cost of credit, so you fully understand your obligations in both the short and long term.

It is important to reiterate that just because you're in negative equity, this does not make you ineligible to obtain another mortgage once your own income can sustain the new borrowing and meet the relevant lending institutions' credit policy.

CHAPTER 14

EQUITY RELEASE

What is Equity Release?

Simply put, equity is the difference between the current value of your house and the amount you owe on it. For example, if your home is worth €300,000 and your remaining mortgage capital is €180,000, then you have €120,000 of equity in your property.

Equity release, therefore, is the 'releasing' of some of this equity. This sort of scheme can be appealing to older home-owners, for example, who want to free some of the equity in their home to fund retirement or an investment.

There are different types of equity release.

Normal Equity Release

A typical example is the case of John and Triona, who can release equity of up to 80% of the current value of their property, which is €240,000 less the outstanding loan amount of €180,000, leaving them with €60,000 equity. Some lenders will usually require documentation to confirm the purpose of the equity release but can consider releasing equity for the purpose of home improvements, educational expenses or the purchase of a holiday home. Each lender's policy is different with regard to equity release, so it is worth taking expert advice before making any decisions.

Lifetime Equity Release

For applicants who own their own home outright and are typically over sixty years of age.

A lifetime equity release scheme allows you to release some of the value of your home without having to make repayments, move out or sell your home. One of the conditions is that the homeowner cannot have an existing mortgage on their home.

Lifetime equity release schemes may be worth considering if you need to raise a lump sum or a regular income in your retirement, and want to continue living in your home. The biggest factor to consider is that releasing equity means that you will not be passing on the full value of your home to your family or other beneficiaries after your death.

This product is currently not available from mainstream lenders, though its legacy remains from its previous availability in the Irish market, and we expect that it will continue to be presented as a niche product offering. The way it worked is that a borrower would obtain a lump sum loan amount of, for example, €100,000 and that the interest payable on this amount (which would usually be higher than the market interest rates) would compound up annually. The total amount outstanding on the demise of the borrower or the sale of their property would be repaid to the lender and any remaining surplus from the net proceeds of the sale would be released to the borrower's estate.

A small number of firms in Ireland offer equity release schemes. Check that the company you deal with is regulated by the Central Bank – there's a section on the regulator's website explaining this area. Since 2008, all companies in Ireland that provide lifetime mortgages or home reversion schemes must meet the conditions of the Central Bank's Consumer Protection Code and must inform you about the costs and risks of taking out an equity release product.[1]

It's important to keep in mind that, generally, equity release can be more expensive than a standard mortgage.

Lifetime Mortgage

A lifetime mortgage is when you borrow money secured against your main residence, while retaining ownership. Generally, borrowers who avail of this type of mortgage are sixty-five years or older. In some cases, you can choose to ring-fence some of the value of your property as an inheritance for your family. The home still belongs to you and you're responsible for maintaining it.

Reasons why someone would take out a lifetime mortgage would be based on their need for funds while being ineligible

---

1   Central Bank of Ireland, 'Consumer Protection Code', https://www.centralbank.ie/docs/default-source/regulation/industry-market-sectors/brokers-retail-intermediaries/guidance/consumer-protection-code-v4.pdf?sfvrsn=4.

for standard loans under typical lender credit policy criteria. So, examples of why they would do so could include their wish to provide a cash gift to an adult child, to purchase a holiday home or to fund medical expenses or a holiday of a lifetime.

Interest is charged on your borrowings, which can be repaid or added onto the total loan amount. When you die or move into long-term care, your home is sold and the proceeds of this sale are used to pay off the loan. For lifetime mortgages, there is no fixed 'term' or repayment date.

If you take out a lifetime mortgage you will typically be charged a higher rate of interest. Safeguards can be offered as part of the product; these include a fixed interest rate for the life of the plan.

Home Reversion Scheme

With a home reversion, you sell all or part of your home in return for a cash lump sum, a regular income, or both. Your home, or the part of it you sell, now belongs to someone else. However, you're allowed to carry on living in it until you die or move out – but you do not have to pay rent. Home reversion plans will usually offer you a value that is well below the market value of your home. However, the older you are when you start a home reversion scheme, the higher the percentage you'll get of your home's market value. You retain the right to carry on living in the home under a lifetime lease. The terms of the lease will vary depending on which reversion you choose.

Fees and Charges

When exploring your potential equity release options, remember to include fees and charges in your calculations. The value of your home will determine the amount of money you can get through an equity release scheme. It's advisable to get a second independent valuation completed in addition to that arranged by the equity release scheme provider to ensure that the valuation the bank is using is as accurate as possible.

Some companies have a fixed 'set-up' fee to cover legal and valuation fees. Some may allow you to pay fees through your lifetime mortgage so that you do not need to have this money upfront. However, if you pay fees through your lifetime mortgage, you will pay interest on them, meaning they will cost you more in the long run.

Consider the likelihood that you might need the equity in your home later on, to pay for future needs, for example, like residential care as you grow older. Releasing some of the equity from your home also means you will not be able to pass on its full value to your family or beneficiaries. The Fair Deal Scheme, operated by the HSE, is designed to provide financial support to those needing long-term nursing home care. Assets, such as savings and property, are taken into account to assess how much the care recipient can contribute towards the cost, and the state pays the balance.

If you do opt for an equity release scheme, you will retain ongoing responsibilities in relation to the upkeep of the property. You remain responsible for ensuring your property is adequately insured – you will need to note the lender's or home reversion company's name on the policy. Regardless of which one of the equity release schemes you opt for, you must keep your home in a good state of repair, and ongoing maintenance costs, of an older property in particular, can be significant.

The lender or home reversion company may carry out inspections on your home from time to time and, if they deem that repairs are required, they will either insist they are completed or arrange for their completion and charge you for costs incurred. If you have a lifetime mortgage, repair costs may be added to the amount you owe, so interest would be charged on those costs. Some schemes may prevent you from carrying out home adaptations, such as installation of a ramp, lift or railings, that may reduce the value of your home.

Keeping your Home

Under equity release agreements you are entitled to remain living in your home. However, this is subject to certain conditions. If you move out of your home for six months or more, your lender may insist you sell up and pay off the mortgage. One exemption to this is if your mortgage is joint owned and one owner remains living in the property. If you fail to insure your home, that can be considered a breach of your contract and you may be asked to sell. Finally, if you don't maintain the property to the standard set out by your lender to retain its value, that could be considered a breach of contract. These conditions will be set out in the documents provided by the lender, so it is important to take the time to review and ensure that you're aware of your obligations.

Considerations

Before you decide if an equity release scheme is the right option for you, consider the following:

- Will the money I receive impact on my pension or entitlements to other state benefits?
- What is the full cost of the scheme to me – upfront and ongoing costs?
- Will the scheme provide enough money to pay for any long-term medical and living costs in the future?
- Can I change my mind? Is there a penalty charge if I do?
- If I want to sell up and move later, can the scheme be transferred to another property?

Other alternatives to consider if you need to raise a lump sum or increase your income are:

- Selling your home and moving to a cheaper or smaller one.
- Taking out a different type of mortgage (if you can afford repayments).

    – Renting out one or more rooms.

Equity release schemes, like all financial products, should be carefully considered, to ensure they are the right fit for your needs.

Look into making a will. Discuss it with family members before entering one of the schemes, to avoid delays in sorting out your affairs after your death.

CHAPTER 15

ENGINEER'S REPORT AND SNAG LIST

Your offer on your dream home has been accepted and you can't wait to move in. But wait before you do, slow down and take the time to give the property a second look.

Although the house or apartment may have looked fine during your viewings with the estate agent, you could have failed to spot some unfinished details or defects during your walk around the property.

Don't let your excitement about moving-in day cloud your judgement so that you miss the loose skirting board or uneven tiling in the bathroom. Or overlook evidence of more serious and costly structural flaws such as cracks in walls or ceilings.

I strongly advise you to get a professional to survey the property and compile a report on its condition. You may need a snag list or an engineer's report, depending on the type of property you want to buy.

Which one do I need?

A snag list and an engineer's report can be described as pre-purchase surveys of a property. Both are usually conducted by a registered professional. The main difference between the two is that a snag list is carried out on a property in a new development, whereas an engineer's report is carried out on existing houses or apartments.

Both reports are typically completed following acceptance of your offer and your payment of a booking deposit to the auctioneer or estate agent. By paying the booking deposit you are reaching the stage of 'sale agreed'. This is the first official step in purchasing a property.

The Snag List

The snag list is made during a survey of a newly built property and consists of an inventory of the details that need to be completed or defects to be rectified. It's usually compiled at the end of the building project by a qualified surveyor, engineer or architect.

The report should cover all internal and external areas, including (but not limited to) the garden and driveway, outer walls, roofs and gutters, attic space, central heating system, doors, electrics, ventilation, insulation, kitchen and fixtures, flooring and tiling, bathrooms, windows, walls and ceilings.

There are two types of snag list: a structural snag list, which is carried out by a professional, and a basic one that can be prepared by you as you inspect the workmanship, functionality, unfinished work, etc. My advice is to have both done.

In a structural snag report, items that you may see listed

include work that does not meet building regulations standards or is deemed defective. Services such as heating, gas, electricity and water should also be inspected.

The report will also include additional advice and information to help you to understand structural certificates and other documentation for the property provided by the builder. It should be signed by a registered professional who is independent of the project, usually an architect. It is then sent to you and to the builder or developer, who should complete work on the listed items before contracts are signed.

Why do I need a Snag List?

It may be difficult to get the builder back in to carry out repairs a few months down the line. It's better to get defects fixed now before you sign contracts or make the final payments. Furthermore, despite recently amended regulations that have further tightened up standards in the industry by obliging developers to appoint an independent professional to sign off on completed projects, it is still a prudent move to get your own snag list done.

The Engineer's Report

An engineer's report is a structural observation survey of a property conducted on second-hand properties. Although it's not always compulsory, I encourage you to have the property inspected by a registered engineer.

Depending on the age and condition of the property, your mortgage provider might ask you to furnish them with this report before you can draw down your loan.

You can arrange for an engineer to inspect the property once you have gone 'sale agreed' with the auctioneer. They will examine the structure of the house, making sure it's sound and there are no faults, such as the dreaded subsidence, which you need to know about now, before you close on the sale.

It is a good idea to have the engineer inspect the boundaries of your property at this stage also by comparing the Land Registry map of the property to existing borders, walls and fences to avoid any possible future disputes about boundaries.

An engineer can also provide information and advice, such as if you need to obtain a certificate of compliance for any extensions carried out on the property over the years. They might also advise you to consider engaging a drainage specialist to inspect any issues with drains, septic tanks and heating systems.

Knowledge is power when it comes to buying a property. Armed with a detailed report of the property's defects and potential problems you are in a good position to decide whether or not to proceed with your purchase, if the issues identified are serious enough.

In the event of the latter, the estate agent is obliged to return your booking deposit in full.

Where do I find a Professional?

I advise bringing on board a trusted professional once you go 'sale agreed'. Ask friends and family for recommendations. Engineers Ireland is the professional body for engineers in Ireland. The organisation's website contains a searchable database of members to help you find an engineer in your area or to check if your preferred engineer has the necessary qualifications.[1]

You can expect to pay between €400 and €800 as an estimate, but this depends on the size of the property and on what type of professional you engage.

Ultimately, however, buying a property is one of the biggest investments of your life. The last thing you want is to discover significant problems with your home after you've moved in. The additional expense and time involved in getting an independent report carried out are worth it for your peace of mind.

---

1   Engineers Ireland, 'Member Search', http://www.engineersireland.ie/membership/search-members.aspx.

CHAPTER 16

THE PROPERTY MARKET AND YOU

In buying this book you have taken the first step towards owning your own home. Whether you're a first-time buyer, a trader-upper, a downsizer or a switcher, one thing each category of mortgage applicant has in common is that they're all 'players' in the property market.

Having a clearer understanding of how the market works can help you to determine your options in the long term and whether now is the right time for you to apply for a mortgage.

How the Market works

As a buyer, renter, homeowner or landlord, you do not need in-depth knowledge of the property market to get involved. However, there are a few key things to remember:

- The property market, like any other market, is cyclical. Prices will rise and fall. There will be a boom and while we may not see another bust as dramatic as that of the recent decade, property values will increase and reach a peak before falling, bottoming out and rising once more. How this affects you depends on where you are in your property journey. For example, if you are looking to buy a house in a 'boom time' market, prices will be rising quickly outside your budget.

- On the other hand, if you are looking to sell and perhaps move to another country that isn't experiencing a boom, then you're in a good position. However, if you are already a homeowner with no desire to move, then a rise or fall in prices may not affect you at all. Once you can afford the monthly repayment, and the house and its location suit your current needs, then the value is irrelevant.

- No one can predict, with any degree of certainty, which way the market will go. While economists and industry experts will forecast what is likely to occur, their opinions often differ. So how do you know who to listen to? The short answer is 'you don't'. But you can try to figure out the best options to suit your circumstances with the knowledge you have. I advise you to take a long-term view when it comes to homeownership.

- If you're hoping to buy, then think carefully about the location. Do you see yourself living there in the long term? If you're merely switching lender or interest rate, then consider whether the new repayments will be suited to your future financial situation.

- Seek expert advice. Choosing a property and a related mortgage product is a complex process. There are no prizes for going it alone when it comes to making big financial decisions.

Your Options

You may have an 'ideal' scenario in your head, but life throws us curve balls and the best we can do is to be prepared for the unexpected.

This book deals with the four main property market players. So, what happens if these 'players' don't get what they set out to achieve? My advice is to do your homework to determine what your choices are.

The First-Time Buyer:

You may not secure mortgage approval first time round. Perhaps your credit history was flawed, or you hadn't saved a sufficient sum for a deposit. Now is the time to consider your next step.

If your credit history has let you down, don't despair. It will take time, but you can improve the situation and then reapply for a mortgage.

If you couldn't get enough money together for the deposit, research all of your options. One to consider is the help-to-buy scheme – a government-backed incentive that gives first-time buyers an income tax rebate up to specified limits to put towards a deposit for a new house or apartment or self-build, subject to certain conditions.

The Second Timer:

You need a bigger home or better insulation. But currently you can't afford the type of property you want. You love your neighbourhood and don't want to move out. Perhaps you should consider a renovation of your existing home? Do you have room for an extension? Could you get solar panelling to improve energy efficiency? Could changes made now add to the value of your home when you are in a better position to make a move? I advise you to look at the grant support options that could be of benefit to you.

The Downsizer:

You want to move to a small property for a variety of reasons – perhaps affordability is key. You'd like to reduce your mortgage but in the current market you cannot find an affordable property that meets your needs. You feel stuck. You're approaching retirement and you can't foresee yourself in the same location for the next twenty years. Do you have options? Yes. Perhaps you can just wait until a suitable property comes to market. Or perhaps you can recoup some of your mortgage spend by renting out a room in your current home. Rent-a-room relief allows you to rent out one or more rooms in your own home without paying tax on the earnings, up to a limit of €14,000.

The Switcher:

You want to switch to a better rate. But you were permanent in your employment when you first took out your mortgage; now, three years on, you've left your employer to start up a new business. Perhaps lenders are a little reluctant to offer you a new mortgage with better terms because they don't see your current position as 'secure'. What can you do? Understand that this categorisation by lenders will have a shelf life, it won't last forever. As long as you keep up to date with your mortgage payments and your finances stay relatively stable, then you can revisit the mortgage switch once you have one full year's accounts filed with Revenue.

Regardless of what type of property market player you are, the key is to be prepared for any and all eventualities.

CHAPTER 17

YOUR MORTGAGE FAQS

By now I hope you have a clear picture of the ins and outs of the mortgage process.

In this chapter, I've tackled some of the questions clients have asked most frequently.

What is a mortgage?

Few first-time buyers will buy a property outright and so most will need a mortgage to buy a home. A mortgage is a loan secured against a property. Having a mortgage means that you borrow the money to buy your home and you repay this over an agreed period of time, depending on what you can afford. MyMortgages.ie can offer guidance on the best type of loan for you.

Should I go for a fixed or a variable rate?

That depends on you and the market conditions.

Fixed rate means that the amount of interest you pay is set for a predetermined period of time, typically three, five or ten years. This offers the benefit of certainty – you know exactly how much the repayments will be. It gives you peace of mind, especially in the early years of the mortgage when your budget may be tight, childcare costs may be high and you have considerable outlays setting up your home in terms of fitting it out and furnishings. For some, this certainty is a valuable benefit. This may not be as important to other mortgage holders.

Variable rates can rise or fall in accordance with a number of factors, including the European Central Bank rate. The most common type of variable rate is the standard variable rate (SVR).

You think you might be able to increase your monthly payments or pay a lump sum off your mortgage over the next ten years, thereby reducing your mortgage term, but there may be a penalty for this if you go for a fixed rate mortgage.

Can't decide? Here are some questions to ask yourself:

– Do I prefer certainty?
– Do I have enough margin at month's end to allow for a rise in rate?
– Do I want the flexibility to pay extra off my mortgage when I have it?
– Do I think it's worth paying a little extra for certainty?
– Is it likely that my monthly income will vary?
– Am I good at budgeting?

Note: If you enter a long-term fixed rate mortgage you will have to grin and bear it if interest rates fall and stay low for a time. How-

ever, even if you choose a shorter term, one to three years, it can be difficult to predict what the rates will be when the time is up. This is fine when markets are low but if they rise your repayments could become unmanageable. Of course, one big advantage of being on a variable rate is that there's generally no penalty should you decide to switch or repay early.

Help! I'm on a fixed term contract, but I'm not permanent. Am I eligible to apply for a mortgage?

The short answer is yes. However, there is a 'but'.

As the working world moves towards a flexible model, more and more of us are in positions that don't fit the traditional permanent pensionable mould. Lenders will look at the usual criteria: your financial management, savings record, credit history and ability to pay.

The role and industry you work in will have a bearing too. Lenders tend to prefer areas such as pharmaceuticals and technology.

Keep records of previous contracts and documentation that demonstrate future opportunities in your field.

Get supporting documents in place. Lenders' requirements may vary, but generally, you will need:

- Two years of financial accounts.
- Six months of bank statements.
- Two years of tax returns.
- A tax clearance certificate.

Should I overpay?

I recently received a promotion at work, which means a considerable bump in my salary. I can easily afford to pay an additional €300 monthly towards my mortgage. I'm hoping to pay it off early and retire by fifty-five. But with interest rates low at the moment, friends have told me to invest the extra cash instead. Should I overpay my mortgage?

Historically, mortgage contracts were for twenty to twenty-five years and typically ended around retirement time. Borrowers tended to stay with the same lender throughout the term of their mortgage and it was rare to pay off your mortgage early unless you were selling the property. However, the mortgage revolution of the past two decades has changed the landscape. And for the better, I believe.

Check with your lender or broker to see if overpaying makes sense from a financial perspective.

When interest rates are low, it may be wiser to invest your extra income elsewhere. However, deposit rates are also low, so putting your money into your mortgage may be a good move.

Sit down and do the calculations. If you will make more by putting the same amount into stocks or shares, you may want to stick with the mortgage repayments you have.

On the other hand, if you'd like to take early retirement and have your mortgage paid off sooner rather than later, and you do have the means to overpay, you can wipe years off the term and save thousands of euro in interest.

Let's look at an example:

Mary takes out a mortgage for €250,000 over thirty years at 3.25% monthly repayment, which works out at €1,088. However, she has recently received a salary increase and can pay an extra €200 off her mortgage per month. If she continues this additional repayment, Mary can cut seven years over the term and save €36,487 in interest.*

Mortgage €	Term	Current Interest Rate	Monthly Payment €	Monthly Overpay €	Term Reduction	Total Savings €
250,000	30	3.25%	1,088	200	84 mths	36,487

* used MyMortgages.ie calculator

Are rent payments taken into account?

I've been renting privately for over a decade and paying premium prices to live within a commutable distance to work. But because of this, I haven't saved a lot. However, if I'm approved for a mortgage for a house in the same area, my repayments will be considerably lower than what I've been paying in rent. Will lenders take this into account when assessing my capacity to pay?

Yes. If you have written records of rental payments going back over the last few years, this will certainly work in your favour.

Along with income levels, credit history and deposit, lenders look at your ability to pay. They work this out using a stress-test model.

Your rent payments plus your savings (these should be regular and not sporadic) should match or exceed the stress-tested payment. This is typically the monthly payment you would pay if your application was approved, with a few percentages added to allow for rises in interest rates.

If you're not already doing this, open a savings account and start making regular payments into it. The bank will prefer regular small deposits rather than larger ad-hoc amounts.

Make sure your rent payments come out of your bank account and are clearly outlined in your statements.

Do I need to know what house I want to buy before applying for a mortgage?

No. You can talk to us today, or use our mortgage calculator, to see what kind of loan you can get. Once you have that, you know what price bracket you need to start shopping in.

How does mortgage interest relief work?

First-time buyers used to be able to get mortgage interest relief, also known as Tax Relief at Source (TRS), for the first seven years. It is calculated by your lender and paid into your account, so if you owe €100 interest and you are on a TRS rate of 25%, you will only pay €75. The rates are usually 25% in the first two years, then 22.5% in years three to five and 20% in years six and seven.

This scheme is not currently available for new borrowers, however. Log on to www.revenue.ie, contact the Revenue Commissioners or call 1890 463 626 for more information.

Can I change my home insurance provider?

Yes and you should notify the insurer of your mortgage as the insurer will need to note your bank's interest on the policy.

What documentation will I need for a mortgage application?

Each lender has its own application form and information criteria, but generally you will need the following:

- Photo identification.
- Proof of address.
- Marriage certificate (if relevant).
- Certificate of income – to be completed and stamped by employer.
- P60 or tax balancing statement for previous year.
- Payslips – three if paid monthly, six if fortnightly, thirteen if weekly.
- Current account statements – previous six months.
- Savings account statements – previous six months.
- Credit card statements – previous six months.

- Loan and/or mortgage statements – previous twelve months.
- Copy of credit history. (See more in Chapter 4.)

Note: Self-employed applicants require additional paperwork. Have a look at Chapter 5 for more information.

What does Annual Percentage Rate of Charge (APRC) mean?

A lender is always required to quote the APRC when advertising a loan or the borrowing rate and its purpose is to help you compare the true cost of borrowing. The APRC calculates the total amount of interest that will be paid over the entire period of the loan. For example, a loan with an interest rate of 3.15% variable over twenty-five years has an APRC of 3.21%.

What is a top-up mortgage?

This is an additional loan given by the lender to an existing borrower on the same mortgage security. The loan 'tops up' an existing mortgage to a higher level. This is commonly used for home improvements.

What other costs can I expect when taking out a mortgage?

There are external costs involved in buying or selling a property, which could include:

- Stamp duty, if applicable.
- Legal fees to your solicitor.
- Valuation report, payable to the bank's valuer.
- Surveyor's report, if applicable.
- Estate agent fees.
- Mortgage protection premium.
- Home insurance premium.

Do I need to be employed to apply for a mortgage?

You'll need to be employed or self-employed to qualify for a mortgage. This will help to ensure you can manage your mortgage repayments in the future. For more information, see Chapter 2.

How do I know if I'm earning enough for a mortgage?

MyMortgages.ie will help you to work out if you can afford the mortgage you need by looking at your household expenditure and any additional financial commitments such as loans, overdrafts, credit cards, hire purchase agreements, personal contract plans (PCPs) and maintenance payments.

Can I get a mortgage offer before I find my property?

Yes, you can obtain approval in principle even if you have not found a property yet.

What other costs may I have when taking out a mortgage?

It's important you add up all the costs involved in a mortgage, not just the interest rate. For example, you may need to budget for a valuation fee, search fees, Land Registry fees and legal costs, as well as stamp duty.

How do I know if the property I'm buying is worth the money?

This is why a valuation report is necessary as it will determine the market value of the property based on its condition, location, comparison with recent sale prices of similar properties in the same area and local amenities.

Do I always need to take out a life cover with a mortgage?

Yes, talk to your mortgage broker about your life cover needs.

When will I know if my mortgage application has been successful?

When we've received all the required documentation and the bank of choice is selected, you should receive approval in principle in one to two weeks. This varies and can take longer with some banks.

What happens after my mortgage is approved?

Your solicitor will carry out various legal checks on the property to make sure they're happy. If there are no concerns, they'll confirm the start date of the mortgage and when they'll need the funds to be released. The funds are then sent to the solicitor who will complete the transaction.

Once the mortgage is approved the bank will confirm how much your monthly payments will be and on what day of the month they'll be paid.

How much can I borrow and for how long?

Generally, 3.5 times your annual gross income (i.e. before tax). Term can go to age seventy maximum.

CONCLUSION

There's no doubt that the mortgage process can at first appear daunting. But, if you arm yourself with a little knowledge and lots of expert advice, your journey from preparation to application through to approval and drawdown should be a smooth one.

This book aims to provide you with the information that you need to approach your mortgage preparation, house hunting and mortgage application with confidence.

Don't forget, the recipe for success is planning. Therefore, prepare well so that you get the mortgage that's right for you, then apply, overpay (if possible) and review regularly.

Shop around. Make sure you apply for the lender that's right for you. Always look for the long-term benefit rather than the short-term gain.

Get advice and don't take the easy option, unless it's the best option.

Good luck!

RESOURCES

Central Bank of Ireland – www.centralbank.ie

Citizens Information Bureau – www.citizensinformation.ie

Daft.ie – www.daft.ie

Department of Housing, Planning and Local Government – www.housing.gov.ie

Engineers Ireland – www.engineersireland.ie

European Commission – https://ec.europa.eu/commission

Homeloan Application Form – https://mymortgages.ie/wp-content/uploads/2019/02/AIMA-Mortgage-Application-Form_2019.pdf

Irish Credit Bureau – www.icb.ie

Irish Statute Book – www.irishstatutebook.ie

The Money Advice and Budgeting Service – www.mabs.ie

Mortgages4Her – www.mortgages4her.ie

Myhome.ie – www.myhome.ie

MyLifeCover.ie – www.mylifecover.ie

MyMortgages.ie – www.mymortgages.ie

Office of the Revenue Commissioners – www.revenue.ie

Property Price Register – www.propertypriceregister.ie

Property Registration Authority – www.prai.ie

Residential Tenancies Board – www.rtb.ie

Sustainable Energy Authority of Ireland – www.seai.ie

The Health and Safety Authority – www.hsa.ie

TheMortgageCoach.ie – www.themortgagecoach.ie (where you can subscribe for news and updates)

The Royal Institute of the Architects in Ireland – www.riai.ie

The Society of Chartered Surveyors – www.scsi.ie

Threshold – www.threshold.ie

GLOSSARY

Advance
The amount of the mortgage loan to be issued by the lender.

Annualised Percentage Rate (APR)
The total cost of credit to the consumer, expressed as an annual percentage of the amount of credit granted. This includes all costs involved, such as set-up charges, the term of the loan and the interest rate.

Annuity (or Repayment) Mortgage
Sometimes called a 'capital and interest mortgage'. This is the most common type of mortgage. The monthly repayment is made up of the interest payment and the capital (original loan amount) repayment.

Appreciation
The amount a property has increased in value.

Approval in Principle
This is an offer from the bank that they will provide you with a loan based on the negotiated terms of your application following their review of your financial position. No funds are transferred to you with this approval, but it supports that the

funds will be available to you when needed. The approval has an expiration period, usually six months.

APRC
APRC stands for Annual Percentage Rate of Charge. This is the yearly cost of your mortgage. It includes not just the interest on your loan but any other charges you have to pay, such as a valuation fee. It also helps if you compare like for like between mortgage providers.

Arrears
If you miss mortgage payments, you are 'in arrears'.

Base Rate
The rate of interest set by the European Central Bank (ECB), which tracker rates and lenders' standard variable rates typically follow.

Breakage Cost
Some mortgages (e.g. fixed rate mortgages) charge a fee if you pay back the loan early. This can vary, so check the original letter of approval or terms and conditions for the charge. This is also known as an 'Early Redemption Charge' (ERC).

Broker
A mortgage advisor offering advice on the range of mortgage deals available from various lenders, e.g. MyMortgages.ie. They are experts in the field, have good relations with the banks, and can secure very competitive rates, or offer you a range of

rates, and a recommendation, based on what's available from a number of lenders.

Building Control Amendments Regulations (BCAR)

Set up to achieve minimum standards in building practice in relation to design and construction methods.

Building Control Management Systems (BCMS)

This is the preferred means of electronic building management. It allows you to create, edit and review notices and certificates.

Building Energy Rating (BER)

This is an overall rating on the energy efficiency of a building. It is measured on a scale of A to G, with A1 being the best rating you can get for energy efficiency and G being the lowest.

Buy-to-let/Investment Mortgage

A mortgage for property that will be let by the borrower to tenants as a source of income and investment – the buyer will not live in the actual property. This mortgage may have different conditions than those applicable to owner-occupier loans.

Capital and Interest Mortgage

Sometimes called an 'annuity' or 'repayment' mortgage. This is the most common type of mortgage. The monthly repayment is made up of the interest payment and the capital (original loan amount) repayment.

Capital and Interest Payment

The monthly payment that covers the interest while reducing the total balance outstanding.

Capped Rate

A combination of a fixed rate and a variable rate. The interest rate is guaranteed not to rise above a set level (the 'cap') within the agreed period, but if the variable mortgage rate is below the capped rate then that is charged.

Central Bank of Ireland (CBI)

Its purpose is to serve the public interest by safeguarding monetary and financial stability and by working to ensure that the financial system operates in the best interests of consumers and the wider economy.

Central Credit Register (CCR)

A centralised system managed by the Central Bank of Ireland that collects and retains information about loans of €500 or more including credit cards, overdrafts, personal loans, mortgages, business loans, moneylender loans and loans from local authorities.

CHAPS Fee

A fee to cover the cost of electronically transferring the mortgage funds to the borrower.

Conveyancing

The legal process of buying and selling property. This should be done by a solicitor to ensure the sale is free of issues.

Collateral

The security for a loan is described as collateral. In the case of a mortgage, the property is considered the collateral for the loan – and in the event of default by the borrower, the lender can realise their security by taking back the mortgaged property.

Cost of Credit

The difference between the amount you borrow and the amount you have to pay back, taking into account interest and other charges.

Credit Rating

The rating that lenders put on borrowers based on their credit worthiness – usually dependent on the borrower's credit history.

Deposit

Paid on exchange of the contract – usually 10% of the purchase value of the house, though this can vary.

Deposit Interest Retention Tax (DIRT)

The tax chargeable on all interest payments.

Depreciation

Any decrease in the value of a property, e.g. from falling house prices.

Discount Rate Mortgage

An initial discount is offered, typically for a period of one or two years. In most cases discounted rate loans will be valid for a specific period of time rather than for the entire life of the loan.

Early Redemption Charge (ERC)

Some mortgages, e.g. fixed rate mortgages, charge a fee if you pay back the loan early. This can vary, so check your original letter of approval or terms and conditions for the amount. See 'Breakage Cost'.

Endowment Mortgage

During the term of this mortgage only the interest on the mortgage is paid to the lender. A monthly payment is also made into an endowment policy (a separate investment policy) – the proceeds of which are designed to repay the mortgage debt and also have surplus funds when the policy expires.

Equity

The difference between what a home is valued at and the amount owed on the mortgage.

European Central Bank (ECB)

The European Central Bank (ECB) is the central bank for Europe's single currency, the euro. It sets interest rates for the region. Mortgage interest rates can be affected by changes in the ECB rate; particularly tracker rates linked to the ECB.

Exit Fee

This is an administration fee payable to service providers when you fully repay your mortgage.

Fair Deal Scheme

A scheme to provide financial support to those that need long-term nursing-home care. It is operated by the Health Service Executive (HSE). Assets, such as savings and property, are taken into account when assessing each individual's financial situation. They then make a contribution to the cost of care and the state pays the balance.

Family Home Protection Act

This is an Act that limits the ability of the owner to sell a family home without getting the consent of their non-owning spouse.

First Charge

A mortgage lender takes a first legal charge, which means that if a borrower defaults on mortgage repayments and the property is sold to repay debts, etc., the mortgage lender gets paid before any other interests on the property.

Fixed Rate Mortgage

A mortgage that is charged at a fixed rate for a set period. The rate payable does not change during the set period – regardless of changes in the lender's standard variable rate.

Freehold

You own both the property and the land it stands on.

Gazumping

Gazumping occurs when a seller accepts an oral offer (a promise to purchase) on the property from one potential buyer, but then accepts a higher offer from someone else. It can also refer to the seller raising the asking price or asking for more money at the last minute, after previously orally agreeing to a lower offer. In either case, the original buyer is left in a bad situation, and has to either offer a higher price or lose the purchase.

Guarantor

A guarantor is a person other than the borrower who guarantees the mortgage repayments. Guarantors can help a borrower who has insufficient income to qualify for a mortgage.

Help-to-Buy Scheme (HTB)

This incentive is designed to assist those saving money for a deposit for their first home. It allows first-time buyers to gain a foothold on the property ladder. This is subject to application and eligibility criteria. (See Chapter 5.)

Home Reversion Plan

You sell a portion of your home to an equity release provider for less than its market value. Then, whenever you sell your house, the profits are split based on your ownership and that of the equity release provider.

Indemnity Bond

A fee required by some lenders where the amount of the loan exceeds 75% of the value or purchase price of the property – whichever is lower. The lender then purchases insurance, which covers them in the event of the borrower defaulting on the mortgage and the lender making a loss on possession and resale of the property.

Inducement

An incentive used to encourage an individual to avail of a product or service.

Interest Only Mortgages

With an interest only mortgage, the mortgage loan is not paid off during the mortgage term, but instead just the interest is paid to the lender and the original amount borrowed is paid in full at the due date of the loan term. An interest only facility can also be arranged for a given term, e.g. one year. In this case, the borrower only pays the interest for the first year and the full mortgage balance will still be outstanding after the interest only period. Generally, after this period, repayments will increase to include capital and interest so that the loan is repaid within the overall term of the mortgage.

Irish Credit Bureau (ICB)

Formed in 1963, the ICB is owned and financed by its more than 300 members, which are mainly financial institutions. The bureau's database contains information on the performance of credit agreements between lenders (i.e. banks and building societies) and borrowers. Information is held for five years after a credit agreement is concluded. The ICB records may assist the lender to decide on the credit it offers. The ICB does not have decision-making power.

Joint Applicants/Joint Mortgages

This is where you hold property ownership rights equally with another person or persons. If one person dies, ownership reverts entirely to the surviving person or persons. This legal agreement supersedes any will the deceased may have made.

Land Registry

The official body that holds the details of property ownership in Ireland.

Leasehold

This is when you own the property but not the land it is built on for a specific number of years. Flats are usually owned on a leasehold basis. You may find it hard to get a mortgage if there are fewer than seventy years left on the lease of the property you want to buy. Leases are renegotiable, but the shorter the remaining term, the more expensive it will usually be.

Letter of Loan Offer

Once a mortgage application is approved, a formal letter of loan offer is sent to the borrower setting out the conditions of the loan. The borrower's solicitor will also receive a copy with a request to proceed with the legal formalities.

Life Assurance/Life Insurance

Life insurance covers borrowers for a set term. Life assurance covers borrowers for their whole life. The Consumer Credit Act requires lenders to ensure that adequate life cover is put in place sufficient to cover the capital and clear the principal amount outstanding.

Lenders require confirmation that the life policy is in place before the drawdown of the mortgage. Life cover provides the funds for the mortgage loan to be paid off in the event of the borrower's death. MyLifeCover.ie offer excellent policy options.

Lifetime Mortgage

When you borrow money against your home, providing it is the main residence you live in and that you retain ownership. Then, when you die or move into long-term care, the money from the sale of the house will be used to pay off however much of the lifetime mortgage is left.

Loan-to-Income (LTI)

LTI relates to how much money an individual can take out on loan from the bank based on their gross annual income.

Loan-to-Value (LTV)

LTVs are shown as percentages and represent the relationship between the size of the mortgage and the value of the property, e.g. a mortgage of €180,000 on a property valued at €200,000 would be shown as 90% LTV.

Local Property Tax

This is a self-assessed tax charged on the market value of residential properties in the state. People liable for this tax must pay it on an annual basis.

Lock-in Clause

This relates to fixed, discounted or capped mortgages, and the penalties associated with breaking the lock-in clause. It is usually attached to special deals and rates and may contain a clause that stipulates the borrower cannot repay a loan prior to a specified date.

MABS (The Money Advice and Budgeting Service)

This is Ireland's free and confidential money advice service. It offers financial review services and expert guidance to those experiencing problems with money management and debt.

Maturity Date

The date the mortgage must be repaid in full, or by which a new agreement needs to be taken out.

Monthly Repayment

The amount you pay to your lender for your mortgage each month.

Mortgage

A long-term loan secured against the borrower's property to finance the purchase of a property. Derived from a French word meaning 'death pledge'.

Mortgage Term

The agreed length of time taken to make the full repayment of the mortgage. Mortgage terms can range from five to forty years.

Mortgagee

The lender providing the mortgage.

Mortgagor

The buyer who takes out the mortgage, i.e. the borrower.

Negative Equity

When the value of the property has fallen below the outstanding mortgage debt.

Offset Mortgage

A lending arrangement whereby the mortgage is linked to the borrower's savings with the same lender. The savings balance is used to reduce the amount of interest charged on the mortgage.

Overpayment

This is when you pay extra, over and above your monthly mortgage payment. You could choose to make a one-off lump sum overpayment or overpay a regular amount with your normal mortgage payment. Overpayments save you interest and will shorten your mortgage term. People often do this as their salary increases or if they come into money, e.g. inheritance.

Portability

Where an existing mortgage can be transferred between properties when you move house.

Payment Holiday

This is a period during which you make no payments on your mortgage. While you make no payments, interest will continue to be charged. This feature is usually only available on some mortgages. Refer to your terms and conditions to see if it's an option open to you.

Pension Mortgage

During the term of this mortgage only the interest is paid monthly to the lender, with the principal due in full at the end of the mortgage term. Contributions are concurrently being paid into a pension scheme. At retirement the tax-free sum can be taken from the scheme to pay off the mortgage.

Pre-approval

When a lender gives approval in principle for a mortgage loan amount. The approval is based on income and other details from the applicant and is subject to certain conditions.

Principal

The sum of money borrowed from the lender – generally what is owed, not including the interest.

Rebuild Costs

The amount it would cost to rebuild your home if it is destroyed (by fire for instance). This is needed for insurance purposes and there are standard calculations to work it out.

Redemption

When a mortgage is paid in full – including interest to date and all charges. This usually occurs when moving to another property or when the end of the mortgage term is reached.

Redemption Penalty

An additional charge made by the lender if the mortgage is fully repaid within a pre-agreed period of time, e.g. if the mortgage is at a fixed interest rate and is paid off in total before the end of the mortgage term.

Remortgage

A process in which the mortgage on a property is moved from one lender to another.

Repayment Holidays

Repayment holidays allow you to spread your monthly repayments over a shorter number of months, for example, ten months instead of twelve, or postpone repayments for a time, for example three months. If you arrange to pay your mortgage over ten months, your repayments will be higher to cover the cost of the skipped months.

Service Fee

The fee charged by a lender who, with the customer's written consent, requests details from their existing mortgage lender.

Stamp Duty

This is a tax payable on the transfer of property. The amount is based on the type and cost of the property and on whether it is a residential or non-residential property.

Split Rate Mortgage

A proportion of the mortgage is set at a fixed rate, and the remainder at a variable rate. If interest rates decrease, repayments on the variable portion of the mortgage decrease as well. If interest rates increase, only the variable payment is affected.

Standard Variable Rate (SVR)

A standard variable rate generally rises and falls in line with changes in interest rates. When the ECB rate rises or falls, the mortgage lender can increase or decrease the variable rate passing on some or all of the rate movement.

Statute of Frauds Ireland

This statute states that the sale and purchase of property in Ireland must be in writing and it also must include details such as where the property is, the price paid and who is involved in the transaction.

Switching

The process of changing mortgage provider to get a lower interest rate on your mortgage with a view to saving money on interest. Usually it involves a mortgage holder switching to a better rate with a new lender to get better value and save money.

Tax Relief at Source (TRS)

Tax relief for home mortgage interest is now provided at source by the lender. Either the lender reduces the mortgage repayment by the amount of the tax relief, or a credit is lodged into the account from which the repayments are made.

Term

The agreed length of time taken to make the full repayment of the mortgage. Mortgage terms can range from five to forty years.

Title

A title confirms who owns a property. There are Land Registry titles, which are registered with the state, and then there are deed titles, which are unregistered.

Title Deeds

Legal documents that provide evidence of the owner's entitlement to a property.

Top ups

An additional loan given by the lender to an existing borrower on the same mortgage security. The loan 'tops up' an existing mortgage to a higher level. This is commonly used for home improvements.

Tracker Rate Mortgage

A tracker rate is a set percentage (margin) above the ECB rate and so it 'tracks' changes in that rate. This margin is guaranteed for the full term of the loan unless there is a material change in the terms of the loan. There is no relationship between the standard variable rate and the tracker rate. A tracker rate may be higher or lower than the bank's standard variable rate.

This interest rate option suits those who wish to avail of a variable rate of interest but want a guarantee on the margin that will be charged for the life of the mortgage. The agreed margin as set out in the customer's loan documentation will not change, even if the bank subsequently introduces a different tracker mortgage offering, at a margin which may be either higher or lower than agreed as per the loan contract.

Valuation Survey

A survey that can be requested by lenders so as to provide an independent professional valuation of the property.

Variable Rate

This means the interest rate can go up or down if your mortgage lender decides to change their standard variable rate.

APPENDIX

Certificate of Income Form

Mortgage Application Checklist

Get Mortgage Ready in 6 Months Checklist

The Mortgage Journey

Dublin – Cork – Galway

Certificate of Income

Employee Name: _____   **Reference:**_____

1 a. What is the amount of his/her **annual gross pay**?   [€ _____]

   b. What is the amount and frequency of any **mortgage subsidy**   [€ _____]

   and/or **Large Town Allowance** and/or **Shift / Rent Allowance**?

   c. What is the amount of   (i) **Overtime** paid per annum   [€ _____]

   (ii) **Bonus** paid per annum   [€ _____]

   (iii) **Commission** paid per   [€ _____]

   annum Are Bonus / Overtime payments **guaranteed**? If not, are   YES ☐ NO ☐

   they considered to be **regular**?   YES ☐ NO ☐

2 Is he/she on your **permanent** staff?   YES ☐ NO ☐

3 Is this position currently subject to a **probationary period**?   YES ☐ NO ☐

4 If yes, please indicate length of probationary period   [_____]

5 Is he/she likely to continue in your employment for some years?   YES ☐ NO ☐

6 **How long** has he/she been in your **employment**?   [_____]

7 What is his/her normal retirement age?   [_____]

8 Is he/she part of a pension scheme?   YES ☐ NO ☐

9 What is the nature of his/her duties?

[_____]

Company / Organisation: _____

   Address: _____

Name: _____   **Company Seal / Stamp (Mandatory)**

Signature: _____

Job Title:_____

Contact Number: _____

Date: _____

Dublin – Cork – Galway

Mortgage Application Checklist

- ❑ Photo Identification – Certified by a Garda/Solicitor/Accountant
- ❑ Proof of Address – Certified by a Garda/Solicitor/Accountant
- ❑ Marriage Certificate – Certified by a Garda/Solicitor/Accountant
- ❑ Certificate of Income – to be completed & stamped by employer
- ❑ P60 for last year
- ❑ Pay Slips – 3 if paid monthly, 6 if fortnightly and 13 if paid weekly
- ❑ Current Account Statements – last 6 months (dated within last 4 weeks)*
- ❑ Savings Account Statements – last 6 months (dated within last 4 weeks)*
- ❑ Credit Card Statements – last 6 months (dated within last 4 weeks)*
- ❑ Loan / Mortgage Statements – last 12 months
- ❑ Pension Policy Document
- ❑ Life Policy Document
- ❑ Income Protection Policy Document
- ❑ Serious Illness Policy Document
- ❑ Copy of credit history – apply FREE online at www.centralcreditregister.ie

****

Also Required for Self-Employed Applicants

- ❑ Signed certified Accounts for the last 3 years
- ❑ Tax Clearance Certificate – both personal & company, where applicable
- ❑ Revenue Self-Assessment – Chapter 4 for last 3 years
- ❑ Form 11 Return Summary for last 3 years
- ❑ Last 6 months business bank statements

****

Also Required for Self-Build Properties

- ❑ Copy of Grant of Planning Permission & Conditions
- ❑ Land Registry Map
- ❑ Detailed costings on bank's template – provided by MyMortgages.ie
- ❑ Copy of Supervising Engineer/Architect/Building Surveyor's professional indemnity insurance policy.

t: **021 4277037** m:**086 8060601**
e:**info@mymortgages.ie** f:**021 4275064**
w:**www.mymortgages.ie**

Directors: Mr. Joey Sheahan   Company Reg. No. 399622

MyMortgages Limited trading as MyMortgages.ie is regulated by the Central Bank of Ireland.

Dublin – Cork – Galway

Get Mortgage Ready in 6 Months

- ❏ Clear your credit cards in full and pay off any amount owing in full every month.

- ❏ Do not use your overdraft even if you have an approved overdraft facility. Keep a minimum balance of €500 in all of your bank accounts.

- ❏ Ensure that you pay your rent by standing order (rather than cash) and that the narrative "RENT" appears on your bank account each month.

- ❏ If you are receiving a gift, ensure this is transferred to you as early as possible.

- ❏ Set up a regular savings account for the required amount – MyMortgages.ie will advise you of the monthly savings amount required. Do not make any withdrawals from this account as this will reduce the amount you qualify for.

t: 021 4277037 m:086 8060601
e:info@mymortgages.ie f:021 4275064
w:www.mymortgages.ie

Director: Mr. Joey Sheahan   Company Reg.No. 399622

MyMortgages Limited trading as MyMortgages.ie is regulated by the Central Bank of Ireland.

The Mortgage Journey.......

1. Send us your details through our website MyMortgages.ie and we will advise what documentation is required.

2. Submit your documentation which can be done by post or emailed to info@mymortgages.ie and one of our Qualified Mortgage Advisors will review and make contact with you.

3. Once all documentation is up to date and in order, your application will be submitted to a bank.

4. The bank may respond with some clarifications which is standard - the sooner we can respond to these clarifications the sooner the bank can make a decision.

5. An Approval in Principle will be issued by the bank once they are happy to lend to you. This can usually take 1-2 weeks from submission of application.

6. We recommend that you apply for mortgage protection life cover before or at this stage to avoid unnecessary delays. Please note that the life cover must be sufficient to cover the loan amount as well as the term of the loan. We recommend adding one year to the term of the life policy in case of any delay closing the purchase.

7. Once you have found a property and have paid a booking deposit please let us know as soon as possible and we will let you know what items are required to progress your Approval in Principle to a formal Loan Offer.

8. At this point, a valuation will be required before the Loan Offer can issue. Each bank has its own panel of approved auctioneers. MyMortgages.ie will arrange the valuation for you. The cost of the valuation is approximately €150 and you pay the auctioneer directly.

9. Once the bank is in receipt of the valuation report a formal Letter of Loan Offer will be issued to you and your solicitor. Your solicitor will advise you on the contents of the Loan Offer prior to you signing same as this is effectively the loan contract between you and the bank. The Loan Offer can take 1-2 weeks to issue after the valuation has been returned to the bank by the auctioneer.

10. We will advise you on the items required for completing the drawdown of the mortgage such as life cover, home insurance etc.

11. Once all conditions have been complied with, funds will be released to your solicitor upon their request to draw funds. Please be aware that it is your solicitor who will advise on the date funds are to be drawn and it's extremely important to confirm this date with your solicitor. Note: It is required to have closing documents into the bank 14 working days prior to the fund release date decided by your solicitor.

t: 021 427 7037
m: 086 806 0601
e: info@mymortgages.ie
f: 021 427 5064
w: www.mymortgages.ie

Director: Mr. Joey Sheahan   Registered in Ireland 399622

MyMortgages Limited trading as MyMortgages.ie is regulated by the Central Bank of Ireland

ACKNOWLEDGEMENTS

This book was only made possible with the support of my family – my wife, Amy Jane, and children, Danny, Abi and Bobby, are the lights of my life and the people to whom this book is dedicated.

I would also like to thank all of those who worked on this book, who brainstormed, cajoled, compiled, researched, calculated, dictated, copy-typed, edited, proofed and spell-checked. I am sincerely grateful for the input of the following who were part of this project: Margaret Balbirnie, Tommy Barker, Kevin Barry, Steven Brown, Paul Bruton, Sinéad Buckley, Jody Cantillon, John Casey, Joe Charles, Willie Clancy, Vincent Clinch, Kerrie Collins, Mairead Collins, Siobhán Coogan, Stephen Coppinger, Ruth Doris, Lyndsey El Amoud, Pat Falvey, Michael Fitzgerald, Pat Fitzgibbon, Declan Fitzpatrick, John Fuller, Fuller Marketing team, Rachel Glynn, Josephine Griffin, Paul Hanley, William Harvey, Terry Hayes, Des Healy, Elizabeth Hegarty, Siobhán Howe, Denis Kelleher, Peter Kiely, Michael Knowles, Damien Long, Ciarán Lynch, Rachel Maher, D. and A. McCarthy, Wayne McCarthy, Daire McGirl, Michael McGrath TD, photographer Daragh McSweeney, Tara McSweeney, Mercier Press, Mortgages4Her team, Norma Murphy, MyLifeCover.ie team, MyMortgages.ie team, Caitriona Nee, Mona Noone, Aidan O'Callaghan, Gerard O'Callaghan, Patrick O'Donoghue, Dave O'Donovan, Noel O'Regan, Dr Dominic O'Sullivan, Trevor O'Sullivan, Cathal Parkes, Jim Power, Damien Quigley, Frank Quinlan, Shirleen Rigby, John Riordan, Sinéad Ryan, my mother Catherine Sheahan, Frankie Sheahan, Jonathan Sheahan, Professor Patrick Sheahan, Vincent Sheahan, Mairead Smith, William Sullivan, Lawrence Sweeney, Kieran Tansey, Caroline Treacy, Marianne Walker, Alison Walsh, Charlie Weston and Kevin Wilson.